God and You: All That Is, All You Are, and Everything In Between

by Jennifer C. Podolak

ISBN: 979-8-9998222-2-2
Printed in the United States of America

Table of Contents

Dedication

This book is dedicated first and foremost to God, I love you eternally.

This book is also dedicated to the ones who cracked open instead of closing.

To the seekers, the feelers, the wounded, the wild, the wanderers, the ones who never stopped asking why.

For the souls who came to Earth to remind and to restore, this is for you, thank you.

Foreword

What are you? What is your purpose? Who are you meant to become? Why are we here? How do we heal, release trauma, or understand the deeper meaning of pain? What are chakras? What are all these random dreams about? Are they even random? If these questions have crossed your heart or your mind—even just once—then it is my honor to welcome you into this living transmission. You already know of these truths from past lives, soul memory, or a quiet knowing that lingers just beyond the veil. Regardless of how you arrive, whether you're coming, going, or here to stay, this work is meant to be a companion on your path, a guide back to the center of you, of all that is.

Throughout life, we are met with countless moments that shape us, launching us forward into our higher versions of ourselves, or looping us through cycles until we're ready to break free. No matter the path, the destination is always the same, back home to God.

What if healing wasn't something we chase, but something we remember? What if the journey of awakening isn't a straight line—but a spiral, a song, a sacred return?

This book is not just something to read, it's something to be felt. It is a living transmission. A vibrational guide. A soul conversation between you and the Divine. These pages are encoded with truth—not just my truth, but yours, too. You would not be holding this book unless something inside of you already remembered.

My name is Jennifer C. Podolak. I am a healer, a channel, psychic, medium, a light worker, a seeker, and what I like to call a bridge. A bridge between the seen and the unseen. I have walked through the valleys of loss, climbed the mountains of remembrance, and laid down beneath the stars always seeking to know more.

Through a series of initiations, awakenings, and dreams, the infinite connection between God, us and all there is became evident. This book is the unfolding of that journey.

Whether you are just awakening or have walked lifetimes with Spirit, this is a homecoming. Together, we'll explore the subtle realms of energy, the sacred architecture of the body, the codes of numbers and sound, and the ancient maps buried within thoughts, dreams, and emotions.

This is your divine remembrance.

How It All Started

For as long as I can remember, I have always loved being outside. I felt like I needed it. I had to be outside for at least a little bit each day. Some of my earliest memories were of my older sister, Jessica, and I playing outside. Whether kickball, playing in our plastic pool out back, or manhunt with our friends on our block in Jersey City. We lived on a small street–Troy Street–and I mean really small street. Although that's not how I remembered it as a child, it stretched for at least a mile for my little legs. It felt like it took FOREVER to reach the park at the end of our street, Pershing Field Park. I also remember waiting for my dad to come home from working in the city. I would wait excitedly at the end of the street, on the corner of Summit Ave and Troy St., anticipating seeing his face and then running into his embrace. He would always greet me with a piece of candy, a Butterfinger usually, and he would ask me about my day as we walked home together exchanging smiles while I ate away at my candy. We lived at the top of the street, right before it did a funny turn, next to a reservoir. Literally right next to one, which I believe also plays a significant role in the supernatural experiences I had as a child.

My older sister and our three best friends from two houses down, Dina, Angie, and Shaddy and I, would crawl under the pointy iron fence to wriggle our bodies behind the reservoir guard building and run as fast as we could down the gravel road on multiple occasions.

Why might you ask? They were building a school at the end of the gravel road and built the playground first! So, of course, we HAD to play on this playground. It was BRAND NEW and your hands didn't burn from gripping the chains on the swings. Could you really blame us? We were just being kids, we weren't causing any harm, we just wanted to adventure.

I fully embraced every chance I had to be outside. Climbing on trees, laying in the grass staring at the clouds, playing manhunt, jumping double-dutch, playing kickball, and riding our bikes around the block. I loved every moment of it. I felt safer outside than I did in my own house, especially at night, so I always begged to stay as long as possible. Once I heard my mom yelling from the porch to come in, I would just brace myself and force myself to walk home. Dreading the moment my mom would close the door after tucking us in for the night.

We lived in a small two-story, single-family home. There was a closed-in front porch, and when you entered the front door there were three ways to go: to the left up the stairs to the second floor where the bedrooms were, straight ahead was the hallway to the living room, and on the right was the dining room which also had its own entrance to the living room. I have fond memories of my sister and I chasing each other through the hallway, into the living room, and then running through the dining room back into the hallway. It was a normal house for everyone, except for me.

The paranormal experiences started when I was a child, I can very clearly remember events as if they happened yesterday. These supernatural events were only happening to me, even though I shared a room with my older sister. As a child, I could not understand or even begin to comprehend what was happening or why I was the only target.. It wasn't until I was much older that I was able to fully process these experiences in greater understanding since I was able to view them from a higher perspective.

During the day, the paranormal activity was relatively quiet, except for an unexpected push down the stairs every now and then. A memory which was brought to the surface almost 30 years later while discussing my neck MRI with a highly intuitive dear friend of mine. I was suffering with neck pain for quite some time, I figured it was from my body mechanics while massaging. I tend to really get into my work sometimes and do catch myself in some peculiar positions. One afternoon in Frenchtown, I had asked her to tell me what she felt when tuning into my neck. She closed her eyes, took a deep breath, looked at me and asked if I had ever been pushed down the stairs as a child? My eyes widened as the memories returned.

On multiple occasions I would walk down the first three steps from my bedroom door to head downstairs. It would lead to a larger corner step, once I would turn and try to step forward, I would feel myself get shoved from behind, causing me to tumble down the stairs and slam into the wall at the bottom. My parents could never understand why I had such trouble with those stairs. I tried to tell them it wasn't me, but it always fell on deaf ears. They chalked it up to me being clumsy and having a vivid imagination. Even though I was in fact clumsy at times, and did certainly have quite a vivid imagination, it did not explain the paranormal events that would continue to transpire night after night.

My house no longer felt like a home at night. It was a much sinister environment. The paranormal activity began after my mom tucked my sister and I into bed. Even though my sister and I shared a room, I never felt safe. The timing of the paranormal activity varied from night to night; it all depended on how prepared I was, but nevertheless it was inevitable. The variation on the timing was dependent on my state of being, if I was in a good mental or emotional state before bed, it usually started immediately after my mom left the room. If I was prepared and waiting for the activity to start, then it would wait until I let my guard down and try to close my eyes. The level of intensity of the paranormal activity also varied from night to night, but it always started the same way.

Like clockwork, every single night as soon as my guard was down, I could feel a shift in the energy of the room. Sometimes when I started to feel the shift, I would try to annoy my sister with random jokes or nonsense just to keep her awake with me. It seldom made a difference, as soon as we got quiet again, the activity would ignite. I could always sense something approaching from the bedroom door towards my bed at the opposite side of the room. Sometimes it would approach quickly, other times it would tease me with fear as it creeped closer and closer.

Every. Single. Night. As soon as it came right up to my face, I would feel this pressure and crazy electricity on my right ear and then I would always hear the loudest gut-wrenching, blood curdling, agony-filled shriek. As if someone was crying out from being murdered right beside me. It would be so loud, so palpable, that my entire body would light up as a cold chill reverberated through me. I would feel that scream echo throughout my entire body, and there was nothing I could do to stop it.

There were times when I would ask my sister if she heard the scream, or if she was screaming. She would usually respond with, "I'M TRYING TO SLEEP JENNIFER!!" or the typical older sister jargon of "THE ONLY ONE WHO WILL BE SCREAMING IS YOU!!"

Night after night I kept wondering to myself, how was she not hearing the scream or the other spirit led conversations in our room, how was she not feeling the eerie presence, and why am I the only one experiencing this?

What usually followed that blood curdling scream consisted of multiple forms of abuse: physical, mental, emotional, and even spiritual. Instead of feeling safe in my own bed, I was being repeatedly pushed, poked, pinched, and scratched. Sometimes even being lifted off my bed from the force of the blows. This was only a small portion of the physical nature of this torment. I would hear demonic entities ridicule and torment me while being attacked in my bed. There would also be conversations happening around me from other entities present in my bedroom. I was shoved down the stairs repeatedly, thankfully it was never hard enough to cause a fatal injury, but just enough to make me question my sanity and fear for my life. What if my neck snaps and what if I don't wake up? I was the only person in my family experiencing these paranormal events, and I felt completely isolated, targeted, and alone. I had no one to turn to for help because no one believed me.

How could it be that even my sister, who would sleep in the same room as me, was not experiencing this level of paranormal activity? As a child I would go to bed fearing for my life as well as for the lives of my family members, who were clearly completely blind to what was occurring. I knew if I could physically be harmed, then they could too. There was no one available to discuss the matter with, and I did not bring it up to others due to concerns about being judged or ridiculed. Anger and resentment grew towards my family for not understanding what I was going through and not being able to help me. The psychological distress was significant..

Most nights the only way I would fall asleep was out of pure exhaustion from fear. Some nights I could take refuge while I slept with wonderful dreamscapes, but most nights I couldn't. This is where the torment continued on an energetic/spiritual level in the astral realm.

My dreams have always been an active place. I can remember the rainbow lights that would appear when I closed my eyes before bed as a child. This may have sparked a memory within you. I have always dreamt in color, more color than we see on this plane. I have always had prophetic dreams, dreams of future events or people which come to pass exactly as in the dream. I have always been able to lucid dream; this is when you are conscious in your dream and are able to manipulate it. I have revisited past lives and experienced traumatic past-life death experiences to be cleared for myself and others. I also have been in communication with other realms and dimensions, being granted access to learning in the astral realm, just as many of you are too. I also meet with councils and guides for myself and the collective while dreaming. Dreams have always fascinated me, and from a young age, I felt that our dreams were a tool for our souls to utilize to help us navigate each lifetime.

Some dreams would mimic what I was watching on TV or recent movies that I had seen. My sister and I watched cartoons and children's shows—mostly, Nickelodeon, Cartoon Network, and Looney Tunes -, this was the early 90's. In my opinion, the scariest shows we used to watch at that age were "Are You Afraid Of The Dark" and "Tales From The Crypt." I had dreamt of the skeleton figure from "Tales from The Crypt" prior to seeing it on TV, and that really freaked me out. The next scariest show for me at that time would have been "Goosebumps." That was the scope of the "scary stuff" that I encountered through TV, which was relatively minimal. The shows I was subjecting myself to were that of basic folk lore and rather light horror/thriller material. These shows were made for children with themes revolving around magic, some folk lore and paranormal phenomena. There were never any episodes of entire families being hung, violently murdered, sexually assaulted, tortured, decapitated, skinned alive, burned alive, et cetera.

Had I been exposed to those types of extremely vile images or depictions as a child, then I would have in fact dreamt of them to process any internal wounds and/or fears around them. If such images were not presented to me through television or media programs, how did they manifest in my dreams, and why were they consistently associated with this particular house? I had more nightmares than happy lucid dreams when living in that house. Coupled with paranormal activity, it felt like the torment never ended. There were nights where the dreams I had were so violent in nature that I was too afraid of even going to sleep the following evening for fear that the dream would continue right where it left off. Night after night I never knew what to expect, all I knew was that it wasn't going to be good. There was one evening in particular that really changed me forever.

When I awoke in the middle of the night one summer evening, something was different. The entire room was ice cold. All the hairs on my body rose almost simultaneously. A cold chill blanketed the room. All I began to hear was my heart beating. I froze as I came to realize what I was experiencing. My sister is peacefully oblivious to the energy of the atmosphere as she sleeps soundly. The bedroom doorknob began to shake forcefully, I instinctively drew my covers closer to my face in an attempt to protect myself from whatever was about to enter the room. Waiting anxiously, unsure of what was to come, when suddenly the shaking stopped.

14

I gripped my sheets as tight as I could.

The doorknob started to turn. It felt like everything was happening in slow motion.

The door swung open, I quickly ducked, covering my face, hoping this was just a dream I would soon wake from. "It's just a dream, it's not real. You're not really here, Jen," I told myself as I waited, feeling time drag on.

After a moment, everything fell silent. There's nothing, no movement, no weird cold static energy, just silence.

"I think I'm safe," I muttered, slowly peeking out to check if anyone was around. Pretending to be invisible, I gently slid my blanket off my face to expose my eyes. I was careful not to move any bit of my body while I slowly turned only my eyes to the bedroom door.

A massive wave of relief washed over me as I surprisingly saw nothing standing before me or the bedroom door. "I knew it was just a dream," I reminded myself and I finally began to relax back into my bed. Just before going to sleep, I noticed the open door. Deciding to close it, I got out of bed slowly.

As soon as I was ready to get up, BANG! The bedroom door slammed shut. Absolutely shaken, I plunged back under my covers. I started to feel myself being poked and pinched from all directions. I started pleading and praying for it to end. I felt something on top of me, pinning me to my bed, it started to suffocate me through my blanket. I then heard that blood curdling scream, my entire body lit up with chills as fear surged through my veins. Suddenly my body and blankets were released and I heard my bedroom door slam shut. I stayed awake as long as I could after that incident only falling asleep from pure exhaustion yet again, as I was too afraid it might come back a second time.

Upon waking the following morning, I proceeded to locate my mother. I decided to ask her why she checked on me in that manner last night, which was my attempt to rationalize what I experienced. If I could get my mom to admit that it was in fact her who opened my door last night, then I could write off this entire experience as just that.

I found my mom in the kitchen washing dishes, without hesitation I asked her why she checked on me last night. She looked absolutely confused at this point, so I continued and said, "It scares me when you open and close my door at night when I can't see you, so next time can you come in to kiss me goodnight instead?"

"Honey, I did not check on you last night, I actually had such a great night's sleep," my mother responded. Well, that was not the answer I was searching for, so in my quest to explain what I experienced I decided to approach my grandmother in the same manner. Now mind you, my grandmother had a bed set up downstairs, she would not walk up the stairs unless she was spending the night in our room. The only time she slept in our bedroom with us was if me or my sister were sick. She was from Poland, and she did not speak much English. I found her in the dining room and asked, "Grandma, you come upstairs at night to my room and open the door?" She looked dead square in my eyes, I could feel my stomach start to knot, and without hesitation she said, "NO!"

I could see in her eyes she knew what I was going through, and when she said no, my entire body lit up like the Rockefeller Christmas tree.

I knew in my heart that my grandmother and mother were not the reason for the events the night before, but I was searching for any type of logical explanation for what I had experienced. I was hoping I could somehow pretend that it was one of my family members, but my heart knew the truth. None of the people in that house were up that night. My mother never checked on me, my grandmother never checked on me, and my dad most certainly did not. Yet again, I felt even more alone, isolated, and scared, and there was nothing any of my family members could do about it. I learned a lot during my time in that house. One of the biggest lessons I learned was just because you can't see it, doesn't mean it's not there. Granted, the way in which I learned that lesson was out of pure fear and terror, not grace and love, but the lesson was still learned regardless.

These soul lessons that I started to uncover were not only built by external experiences but also deeply held internal beliefs. I was born into this world with my own beliefs, just as each of us are. However, it was apparent to me, even at a very young age, that some of my beliefs were not conventional.

Between the ages of five and six, I can remember crying upstairs in my room. My mom heard me wailing from downstairs, so she came up to see what I had gotten myself into. When she opened the door and saw me on the floor, she asked what was wrong, "I want to go home, I don't want to be here anymore, I want to go home," I cried. With a puzzled look she said, "I don't understand honey, you are home."

"This isn't my home, I just want to go home!" I exclaimed. "This is your home," she responded. With tears continuing to roll down my face I pleaded, "No mom you don't understand, I am not from here, I want to go home! I hate it here, this isn't my home, everyone is so mean, sad, and so angry. I hate it here; I don't want to be here anymore. **I want to go home!**"

I knew this was not my soul's home. I couldn't explain it any better than that as a child. I also knew my mom did not understand, how could she? She gave birth to me, so for me to say this was not my home would have definitely been a jarring experience for her.

Eventually, the nightly terrors and daily frustrations of not being understood came to a climax. I mentally, emotionally, and physically could not handle all of the paranormal events anymore. Nor could I longer bear the weight of not being listened to or understood. The feeling of being so alone while in a room full of people who were supposed to listen and protect me broke me down. I wanted to be normal, I just wanted to be like everyone else.

One evening before bed I prayed for all of it to stop: all of the visions, the demons, the nightmares, the screams and pokes and prods and pushing, the fear, the isolation, all of it. I prayed to be normal, I wanted it to end, I prayed to feel like I fit in. I wanted to be believed and I wanted to be accepted. My heart was hurting, my soul was yearning, and I just didn't want to feel any of it anymore.

That night would be the last time I saw rainbow flashes of lights whenever I closed my eyes, it was also the end of spirit-led conversations in my bedroom. Eventually the evening scream came to a halt, and the night terrors decreased.

Ironically, we ended up moving from that Jersey City home a few months later, and I was able to start a brand-new chapter of what felt like a world away. First, we moved to Middletown, then to Holmdel shortly thereafter. The paranormal activity was at a standstill, but the nightmares and prophetic dreams remained. I was still mirroring people's emotions, while downloading them into me as my own, but I felt more normal. The most significant change I noticed was an increase in headaches; I would get at least one headache a day which would sometimes evolve to migraines. The migraines were debilitating- I physically had to shut down every time a headache turned to a migraine. No lights, no sound, no smells, cold pack over my eyes and head- I had to be left completely alone.. If I didn't get to rest fast enough when the migraine started, it would lead to vomiting and full body convulsions. The headaches did cause me some issues in school while attending St. Benedicts in Holmdel. I had trouble focusing when they started and I had learned that my classmates and teachers did not believe that I was actually experiencing headaches.

One afternoon while in seventh grade on a day where we had a substitute teacher, I asked if I could be excused from class to go to the nurse for my headache. She kindly agreed and I went to the nurse. The nurse would give me a frozen towel ice pack and I would lie there for about 15-20 minutes. Once my headache subsided, I would return to class and continue on with my day. This time upon entering back into my classroom, the substitute had asked me if I actually had a headache or if I was making it up to skip class because that is what my classmates had told her I do. Hurt by this, I explained to her that I was not lying and that I do get headaches everyday. I also explained that my parents know and they told me to go to the nurse and then back to class once it's over. I knew I still didn't fully fit in or was normal like everyone else, but the paranormal activity was nowhere near the level it was from previous years, so I just forgave them, let it go and did my best to be happy.

A few months later I was invited to a sleepover at one of my friend's houses for her thirteenth birthday, it was a small gathering since everyone there was going to sleep over. At one point during the evening, a Ouija board was brought out. I had never seen one in real life before but always had a terrible gut-wrenching feeling about them. I begged them not to play with it and told them of this bad feeling I was getting, but they just brushed me off and said the Ouija board was just an urban legend. My friend who was hosting had a younger sister, so while the others decided to play with the Ouija board, I decided to play Barbie's with her little sister instead.

In all honesty, it was really hard for me to pay attention to the Barbies with this overwhelming sensation of fear creeping over me. My eyes could not stop darting to the room they were in. It was hard for me to put into words at the time, but, looking back on it, I could sense the danger that they were placing themselves in, and I was frozen in terror. I did my best to block out what happened to me during my childhood in Jersey City, and I most certainly did not want to experience that again, nor would I wish it upon anyone.

I just couldn't understand why they wouldn't listen to me, so I did my best to focus on the Barbie game instead. Not more than five seconds later, I heard a loud BOOM, followed by shrieks of terror from everyone in that room. I ran into the bedroom as fast as I could to make sure everyone's okay. I found them with the lights on, looking as pale as ghosts, so I asked what that loud noise was. Apparently, they had asked the Ouija board if anyone was here, the eyeglass moved to "YES" then every single window proceeded to slam shut at the exact same time!

"I told you this wasn't a good idea, I tried to warn you that something would happen!" I said. We all scurried out of her room; even though I didn't participate I was still shaken. We decided it would be best just to pull an all-nighter because no one wanted to sleep in her room. Off to the finished basement we went to play the night away, and, once the sun came up, we jumped on our opportunity to get on the trampoline.

I was enrolled in competitive gymnastics at the time, coaching classes on the weekend, as well as hosting children's gymnastics birthday parties. I would say I had plenty of experience on a trampoline at that point, and it certainly wasn't my first time jumping with a group. Every kid loves to play popcorn on the trampoline!

There were about five of us on that trampoline, while we were all jumping, I found an opportunity to land in a seated position, a seat-drop.

As I was coming down onto the trampoline, everything switched into slow motion. When my legs were fully extended in front of me, another girl had decided to switch her position underneath me. Had I kept my legs fully extended, I would have landed on her and then been subsequently landed on by someone else, potentially snapping both of my legs from being hyperextended.

I tucked my knees as close to my stomach and proceeded to say, "WATCH O–," but couldn't finish as I nearly bit my tongue in half from the force of me smashing my chin into my knees. I screamed from the pain, my tongue started gushing blood, and I ran as fast as I could to my friend's mom inside. What's interesting to note is that I was the only person to speak out against using the Ouija board, as well as the only person to get injured at the sleepover.

After that sleepover, the paranormal activity started to pick back up around me, not as intensely as it was in Jersey City, but strange events did start to occur every now and then.

I always felt something big would happen on or around my 13th birthday. I was never shown in my dreams what would happen, I just always knew that something would.

I remember being in my room on the day of my 13th birthday. I very much enjoyed my time alone, and as I was sitting on my bed a strange sensation came over me. I felt this sudden urge to speak, not in words, but in tones. I began to speak light language. To my logical mind it sounded almost like alien gibberish, but in my heart, it felt as if I had heard this before. It activated a remembrance deep within me.

The moment I stopped speaking the light language transmission, my entire room became completely blurry. Everything in the room melted together just like a beautiful tapestry. There was no beginning and no end to the objects around me. Once I was fully aware of this, everything started to become clear again. Not just kinda clear, I mean crystal clear. Colors that I had never seen before started to emanate from the objects in my room. My entire room was glowing.

There was an iridescent crystal overlay outlining everything. The colors resembled an iridescent holographic rainbow mixed with intense silver and white light. I heard a high-pitched ring; chills then reverberated throughout my entire body. I took a deep breath and my bedroom gracefully returned back to normal.

I was in absolute awe, "I bet that's an actual language from somewhere," I thought to myself, and again chills ran down my spine.

That's when I realized the chills are confirmation. The chills are soul resonance.

How am I going to explain this to anyone? Am I even supposed to tell anyone about this, should I even bother? "The time will come," I heard a gentle voice whisper, and so I continued on with my day. My life changed that day on an energetic level and in turn so did my level of consciousness. So much so that it was mirrored to me by my mother on my 13th birthday.

I thought it was strange that I did not receive a birthday gift all day. Especially when my mom would be sure to surprise me and my sisters with our gifts the morning of our birthdays. At about 10:30 PM, I still had not received any birthday gifts, so I chalked it up to my mom forgetting to get me a gift. I sunk into the couch and continued to watch TV, trying to keep my mind off of it.

Five minutes later, she walked right up in front of the TV holding a giant gift with a smile on her face. She said, "Honey, I did not forget you, this is a very special birthday." I started to beam with joy, excitement pouring from my smile. She continued. "Now that you are 13, we will provide a roof over your head, a room for you to sleep in, and a bed for you to sleep on. We will drive you to and from school, and make sure you have enough food to eat. However, now that you are 13, you must get a job. Anything you want you will get on your own—clothes, hair accessories, getting your hair done, makeup, going to the movies, going out with your friends—you are now responsible for it. I wanted to wait until the time of your birth, 10:35 PM, to officially say happy 13th birthday!" My smile completely faded by the time she finished, "You're kidding, right?" I thought to myself, but I knew she wasn't. She meant every bit of what she said, and so transitioned from just learning gymnastics to also coaching gymnastics the following Saturday at Aerials Gymnastics in Eatontown, NJ. As I had leveled up on the energetic level, it translated into my physical reality with my mom telling me I had to start working. I had to take over more responsibility for the world around me.

Gymnastics was my passion; it kept me grounded while allowing me to learn about myself and even life in so many ways. I competed for Rebound, Aerials Gymnastics, and also made the Holmdel High School varsity gymnastics team. I was co-captain of the varsity team my junior year and captain my senior year. I never pursued my gymnastics career after high school. The ankle injury I sustained three days before the Shore Conference Championship my junior year changed the course of my gymnastics career entirely.

During the competitive season of high school gymnastics, we would practice every day after school, and then I would continue my practice three times a week at my home gym until about 9 PM. I had just finished two floor routines during high school practice and asked my coach, Liz Porter, if I could finish up and head over to the uneven bars. The uneven bars was my favorite event, second runner up would be the balance beam. Liz was reluctant and asked me to run through one more floor routine. I had a really bad feeling come over me and my gut told me no. I asked her if I could save that last routine for Shore Conference, but she insisted one more routine wouldn't hurt.

I prepared myself mentally while waiting for my music to start. I opened with a bit of choreography to a jump combo which spun me into the corner. This sequence placed me exactly where I needed to be for my opening pass, a front handspring front layout. I took a breath and started my sprint into my opening pass, I completed my front handspring and I launched into the front layout. Just as my heels passed over my head, I felt my body get jerked to the side. I did a partial twist and landed completely on my right ankle. The weight of the landing caused my body to snap backwards, and I collapsed onto the wrestling mats. I heard Liz scream, she ran over to me, and I saw my best friend run out of the gym. Within minutes the trainer arrived, and I was escorted to the hospital with my mom by my side. My ankle never fully recovered even though I didn't break any bones. I tore the deltoid ligament also known as the medial ankle ligament. A major injury which kept me out of gymnastics for a few months. I returned to gymnastics to finish out my senior year but never pursued gymnastics into college.

After high school I attended Monmouth University. I was a bio major with a focus on dentistry and, instead of competing, I remained coaching gymnastics. It was during my time at Monmouth University that I miraculously found out what actually happened three days before the Shore Conference. That gut feeling I had- not to go for my third floor routine, was me sensing the ill will or ill intentions being sent to me by my supposed best friend. It was my soul warning me of what was going to happen. As it turns out, my best friend at the time—who was the first person to run and get the trainer—only did so because she felt guilty for what happened. She later admitted that she had actually wished that something terrible would happen to me right before I started that very routine. Why would she wish that? Someone had accused me of stealing her Abercrombie gift card and she had been ruminating on that being a possibility instead of coming to ask me directly.

I coached gymnastics on and off until the age of 27, and I truly loved every moment of it. Even though coaching gymnastics brought me so much joy, and I was really good at teaching, I knew coaching wasn't what I was meant to do forever. Yes, I really enjoyed teaching gymnastics, but how did that correlate with my ability to feel other people's energy and emotions? Why did I have the ability to read people and situations? How am I supposed to use these gifts to help others on a deeper level?

I found that I was always searching to go deeper, wanting to know more, and more so wanting to know why. I never really formally started my prayers with God as they did in St. Benedicts or at Church. I just think of God in my heart and speak, so I just asked for guidance, "God show me which way to go, I don't know what to do."

I never completed my degree at Monmouth University; I wasn't built for the classic classroom experience. I never felt like I was actually connecting with the curriculum, and I just always felt like there was more to learn outside of the classroom. My life experiences ended up bringing me to New Hampshire. I had moved up there with a boyfriend who was being relocated for work. I agreed to move up with him since I was planning on spending the rest of my life with him, or so I thought. I already had a coaching interview lined up for me, so I was eager to get started. I also ended up starting and running a decal company on the side for some extra cash.

The hard truth is, unless you own your own gymnastics studio, you're really not going to be making as much money as you deserve by just being a coach. Regardless of how much I loved coaching and the children, I had to make ends meet, so I reluctantly ended my coaching career and headed into the world of corporate America.

I landed a job at Labor Ready, a staffing agency in Concord, where I worked as a customer service representative. It was an extremely repetitive position, very easy and it was steady income. As the months passed, I became restless. I started leaning on alcohol after work, trying to numb the agony of waking up to a miserable existence. I caught myself starting to slip, reaching for the bottle after every shift, descending down the same slippery slope I had also watched my parents descend into.

"What the fuck am I doing and what the fuck is the point of all of this? There is no way God would create us just to have us live like THIS! I KNOW I AM MEANT FOR MORE GOD, I JUST DON'T KNOW WHAT. BUT I AM FUCKING DONE WITH THIS!" I cried to myself one evening as tears soaked my face. I didn't know what I was meant to do, I just knew this wasn't it.

I woke up the next day still in the same position I cried myself to sleep in, unsure of what to do next, but knowing I couldn't depend on alcohol to get me through. As I got myself ready for another dreadful day, I realized what was happening. I had heard of it before but never really understood it. I am going through the dark night of the soul. The period where everything I once leaned upon for comfort or solace crumbles to ash beneath my feet. Anything and everything that could go wrong did.

That boyfriend that I was ready to spend the rest of my life with, well I was sent a photo of his online dating profile the following week while he was away on a business trip. A friend had sent me a screenshot of his Plenty of Fish profile which showed he was actively seeking other women and claimed to be single! He even updated his location to New Hampshire. Not only did I find out that my boyfriend that I left my entire life in New Jersey for was cheating on me, but now I had to find a place to live on my own. When I called my mom to tell her, her response was, "I knew you would never make it on your own." And then she proceeded to unload her concerns about infidelity and my poor life choices, and how I would never amount to anything. It was definitely not the support I needed, my world was falling apart, and it felt like there was nothing I could do to stop it.

I ended up staying in New Hampshire for a few months before I moved back home to New Jersey. I had to prove to myself and to everyone else that I could in fact make it on my own. Remarkably, when it was time for me to move back to New Jersey, they transferred me into a higher paying position within Labor Ready and after that I became a branch manager for a satellite office, Spartan Staffing.

I was making more money which was nice, but I still didn't feel fulfilled. During this time, I ended up moving in with one of my best friends. She was living on her own in Keansburg, had an extra room that she offered to me, and I gladly accepted. What's the worst thing that could happen, right? All I was doing was moving into a house with my bestie.

Everything was pretty normal in that house at the beginning, but then things started to get really weird. I noticed that anytime I went into my room I felt completely drained and would get the feeling that I was being watched. I noticed I really didn't like to be in that house at all and would make any attempt to avoid being there. I was seeing someone at the time, so any chance I had to not sleep at that house in Keansburg I took. It soon became apparent that my friend and I were not the only inhabitants in that house. The only thing is, we couldn't see who else was there, but they definitely made themselves known on multiple occasions.

One evening, myself, my roommate, and a mutual friend of ours were playing cards. The three of us sat at the kitchen table, and from this angle we could all see clearly into the living room and the doors to both bedrooms.

We were playing rummy when, unexpectedly, we all felt this heavy presence, our attention shifted to the living room where we all caught the tail end of a figure out of the corner of our eyes. The three of us brushed it off as a shadow from one of the cats and continued on with our game. It was around 12 AM when my roommate decided to head to bed since she had to be up early for work. My friend and I said goodnight to her and continued to play cards.

As we were playing, we both kept seeing something out of the corner of our eyes, each time our attention was directed to the bedrooms. We started to hear disembodied voices and scratches coming from the doors and windows.

We did our best to ignore what was going on, but we could both feel the tension rising as we continued to play. It started to get late, so I told her I was going to get to sleep; I went to bed and she slept on the couch.

The next day my friend told me she didn't sleep well at all, each time she tried to close her eyes to sleep something would startle her awake. I told her that I really felt uneasy after last night and that I didn't sleep well either. We tried to brush it off, keeping our minds occupied during the day. As the evening approached, we returned back to the house.

My roommate was already home and we gathered once more at the kitchen table. Night fell quickly as the evening went on. My roommate once again went to bed before us. My friend and I decided to stop playing cards and put on a movie. We were getting ready to settle in when noises started to come from the doors and windows. We heard a knock at the front door, it then became more aggressive and sounded as if someone was trying to break the door open. The doorknob of the front door started to shake, and you could hear what sounded like claw marks going down the door.

We decided to investigate what the noise was, as we got closer to the door it became more and more violent. We could hear whispers coming in from all the windows, both of our bodies were on high alert. My roommate was sound asleep in her room, and we didn't want to wake her just in case it was nothing. Although I knew this was definitely something, I did my best not to panic. As we started to walk back to the kitchen something hit the wall behind us, and we watched a figure walk through my bedroom wall and go stand over my roommate.

We looked at each other and immediately started to pray in the name of Jesus. "We need holy water," she exclaimed. We ran to the kitchen sink and blessed it as best we could. We started walking to every room, window, and door to draw crosses on them while saying, "I REBUKE YOU IN THE NAME OF JESUS!"

The more we said it, the more violent it became. The scratching at the door, the whispers, the doorknob, the entire house was stirring. It felt like I was in the middle of the scariest paranormal movie I had ever seen, except this time I was on the receiving end.

Once we blessed the front door, my bedroom was next. I had a puppy Build-A-Bear on my bed that I made when I was 12-years-old.. When you pressed the puppy's paw it said, "I Love You, I Love You," in a very high-pitched, child-like tone. I, without rhyme or reason, put two hearts inside of it, one plain heart and one checkered pattern heart.

Now this stuffed animal was all the way on the far side of the room on my bed. It was not outside of the room; it was inside the room. We could both physically see it on the bed as we were blessing my room. We stood outside of the door to my bedroom, spraying the blessed water everywhere.

Just as I was about to say "I rebuke you in the name of Jesus" for the third time, I heard a demonic voice standing right next to me say, "BUT I LOVE YOU!" My friend, who was standing slightly in front of me, turned around to look at me and said, "DID YOU JUST FUCKING HEAR THAT!" I screamed, "YES, AND IT WAS RIGHT FUCKING NEXT TO ME!"

We were completely stunned, and realized that we did not have the proper training for this type of activity. I told her I would go to the local church the following day to have a priest come and bless the home. We both stayed on the couch that night, there was no sleep for either of us. I got ready and left for work the next day, and, afterwards, I drove straight to the church at St. Benedicts in Holmdel.

I had a feeling that what was in the home was also attached to me. I knew this because every time I tried to pray or speak out against it, my throat would close. I even had three vehicles attempt to push me off of the Driscoll bridge on my way to the church that afternoon. They surrounded my car and started pushing me towards the water. I swerved my car towards the one that was to my left as I slammed on my brakes and managed to maneuver my way around them.

I drove as fast as I could, hoping that I would get pulled over so I could ask for an escort. I made it to the church, and I ran as fast as I could to find the priest. I unloaded everything we had been experiencing in that house, and even things I experienced from childhood. I was shaking and crying, afraid that the torment of my childhood had returned, and I could not bear to go down that road again. The priest asked if I had been baptized and I told him no, at which point he immediately agreed to baptize me even though it was not normal for a person to be baptized in this manner. Once that water hit my head, I felt three whooshes of energy fly off of my body. I felt lighter, but I didn't feel like I was in the clear. The priest agreed to come over later that night to bless the home because he could sense the urgency of this situation. I thanked the priest as I walked back to my car gripping the rosary he had just given me.

Prior to his arrival that evening, the energy of the house started to shift again and become active. I was sitting at the kitchen table with my friend, holding the rosary beads that the priest had given me earlier after the baptism.

I placed the rosary around my neck and began to pray The Lord's Prayer.

"Our father who art in Hea-," was all I could mutter before I started to feel my throat closing. I was being strangled, the rosary beads around my neck started to tighten.

I gathered up as much courage as possible and started again, this time with more emphasis. "OUR FATHER WHO ART IN HEAVEN, HALLOWED BE THY NAME." I got further than before but the beads started to choke me, this time pulling my head and neck down towards the ground.

With even more power and might I began again, "OUR FATHER WHO ART IN HEAVEN, HALLOWED BE THY NAME, THY KINGDOM COME, THY WILL BE DONE, ON EARTH AS IT IS IN HEAVEN! GIVE US THIS DAY OUR DAILY BREAD AND FORGIVE US FOR OUR TRESSPASSES AS WE FORGIVE THOSE WHO TRESPASS AGAINST US IN JESUS'S MIGHTY NAME. AMEN!"

I felt a cold chill run through my body as I concluded, I looked to my friend and then looked at the time, only an hour left before the priest was to arrive.

My roommate came home from work and joined us in the kitchen. Shortly thereafter, the priest arrived and began to bless every room in the house.

He led a prayer to bless all of us after he had cleansed the home, during that prayer I felt another three entities leave my body. I didn't say a word to anyone about it. On his way out, he made sure to grab the Build-A-Bear puppy so that he could dispose of it properly, his entire demeanor changed once he picked it up. Pinching it with the fingers of his right hand, holding it as far away as possible from his body. He was convinced that whatever I had experienced as a child had attached itself to me and then to this stuffed animal, hence the two hearts. Which also explained the incessant need for me to bring this stuffed animal everywhere with me. No matter where I moved, it always came with me, and it always slept in my bed. Whenever I hugged and gave love to that stuffed animal, I was unknowingly amplifying the connection with that entity.

After that stuffed animal and the priest left, the house felt really good. I actually felt comfortable in my room. I moved out of there and back home a short time after. We didn't speak much of the incident to anyone. Quite frankly because who would believe it?

After that experience, the memories from my childhood were starting to flood back in, but this time I was seeing them from a higher perspective. I now had even more questions about my experiences, and I was still searching for where I belonged.

It was a normal Tuesday morning, I was sitting at my desk reviewing the clock-in punches, making sure all the workers were accounted for. All the while ruminating over the purpose of life and everything that I had experienced up until this point, wondering how it all fits together.

I started thinking of my experiences in school growing up, and how it really didn't prepare me for anything that I experienced, nor was it facilitated in a way that was conducive to my style of learning. Then, I realized how I actually ended up learning a lot of life's core lessons by participating in and coaching gymnastics. Suddenly the flood gates opened, and a 26-page business plan titled Action Universe, which focused on the benefits of adding a hands-on curriculum, was born in under three hours. I had never written a business plan in my life. I was enthralled! I thought to myself, this is my purpose, this is what I am supposed to write about!

My intention after that point was to do everything I could to integrate this hands-on curriculum into the educational system for the United States. I boldly decided to send a copy of this business plan to the president himself, Mr Donald J. Trump.

Who the hell did I think I was? I didn't care if I sounded crazy when I told people I was mailing it to the president. I just really deeply knew there needed to be a change and really believed that this could actually work.

I reached out to all the contacts I had hoping to land a foundation for Action Universe, one of which worked for the New Jersey Devils. I sent him over my business plan, and he agreed to meet with me the following week at the Prudential Center in Newark. I was pumped, but also extremely nervous! During our meeting he said, "I want to tell you something. I also teach people how to draw up business plans, and this business plan is the most complete business plan I have seen!" I was shocked. I told him how it all happened and that it was the first business plan I had ever written with no prior experience or training. It was all divinely downloaded. As elated as I was to hear that he really loved my plan, he followed up with "We would be more than happy to have the New Jersey Devils participate in your program once you have your school up and running." I smiled and thanked him for his time, kept my chin held high as I walked out that door, but as soon as I got back to my car I sank.

A whole school? I was just trying to have it adopted into the current ones, not build my own. Defeated, I headed back home, pondering my next step, but also reminding myself to be proud of pushing past my comfort zone. I left corporate America a short while later and returned to coaching gymnastics while I tried to figure out my purpose. On a whim, I decided to mail the Action Universe business plan to the president, Mr. Donald J. Trump, I figured if anyone could get it implemented it would be him. If not, maybe someone would find it and adopt it as their own, I didn't care, I just wanted something to change. I knew my purpose wasn't behind a desk, and I absolutely had no way of opening a school, so I returned to what I loved, coaching gymnastics.

Some time had passed and I was hanging out with some friends. I snapped back from a daydream and focused on my friend, who was speaking. Suddenly, something strange occurred. Out of the blue, I started to feel a circuit of energy flowing from my fingertips in my left hand all the way up my left arm. It passed through my entire chest then I felt it rush down my right arm. I had never experienced a surge of energy run through my body like this before, so I did my best not to make any sudden movements to alarm the people I was with. I had only met these people a few months ago, I was relatively new to the group, so they had no idea about my childhood or previous supernatural experiences. I was always more of an introvert so I usually had a harder time making friends, and I was afraid they might not want to be my friend if I told them what was happening.

Suddenly, one of the girls in the group stopped talking mid-sentence, locked her eyes with mine and gasped. "YOU'RE A REIKI!" she exclaimed. I am sure I looked like a deer in headlights while I stared at her. Half afraid of what she might say next, unsure of where this conversation was going. While also partially amazed that she could feel it, but still also freaked out because that surge of energy was so intense.

She smiled as she said, "You're a natural Reiki, Jen. You're taking my energy, changing it, and giving me back higher energy."

"OMG! WHAT??! ARE YOU SERIOUS?! THIS is why I have had these experiences in life?!" I asked, forgetting that the others in the room have no idea what I am even talking about. At that moment, I didn't care, it felt so good to feel seen and actually understood.

After that initial conversation, I dove headfirst into Reiki and energy work, and I started to shift my entire career path. I stopped coaching gymnastics and decided to dedicate myself to learning everything I could about Reiki, energy, consciousness, and my connection to God.

I received my level one Reiki training certificate in 2016. At that time, Reiki was fairly uncommon in New Jersey. I had to figure out a way that I could get my hands on people. The more people I could get my hands on, the more people I could introduce to Reiki and energy work. This is what drove me to obtain my massage therapy license. I simultaneously obtained my Reiki Master certification and my massage therapy license in 2018.

This living transmission was born through this work. The information that I am presenting in this book is a collection of the information that has been imparted to me during client sessions, which includes bodywork, Reiki, tarot readings, soul guidance, and other forms of energy work. I have also been guided to include transmissions and downloads from my personal meditations, as well as dreams which are meant to serve the highest good of the collective.

It is an honor for me to present this information to you at this time, and my intention is that you receive all that you need for your highest good and for your highest healing. It is also my intention that this book guides you back home, helping you to remember who you are, and how divinely orchestrated your life really is.

God Is

I could begin and end this entire book with those two words alone, because within them lies the whole truth. Yet I know not all will feel that at first glance. That level of recognition–a knowing, really– must rise from within and I can promise you it's there, a deep remembrance waiting to be unlocked.

I. God is All That Is

This truth is the very axis upon which creation turns, and when you begin to see just how far you've drifted from that center, you will also realize you hold the power to return.

II. So, if God is… what are we?

We are the creation of God—reflections of the consciousness of God projecting our consciousness in human form. As extensions of God, our Infinite Creator, we too have the capacity to create; to project and shape our own realities.

Energy, Intention, & Divine Creation

Everything Is—And Has the Capacity to Be—Divine Conscious Energy

Human beings are electromagnetic by nature, we respond to frequencies. Our bodies are quite literally designed to run on energy. This divine current not only animates us but also flows through everything: animals, nature, planets, galaxies, consciousness, and entire multiverses.

Our thoughts, emotions, and actions are expressions of this energy. Some are conscious, born from intention and awareness. Others are unconscious, triggered by trauma or survival instincts. Whether we realize it or not, we are always transmitting energy and the frequencies we emit influence our external reality.

If you believe your day will go well, that belief will magnetize aligned experiences to confirm your belief of your day going well, thus ensuring you experience a day that goes well. If you carry dread or speak negatively towards your self/day/situation, those words ripple through the field and return to you for you to experience that reality. What you send out—through thought, feeling, speech, or action—is what you receive. Some call this karma, others the law of cause and effect. Whatever the name, the truth remains: you are responsible for creating your external reality for it is simply a reflection of your internal reality.

AS ABOVE : EXTERNAL | SO BELOW : INTERNAL

The reflection of where we are at on a consciousness level as well as what our soul would like to know will often manifest in various forms—through emotional, mental, physical, or spiritual events. The people in our lives are our divine mirrors, helping us remember what we came here to complete. Some play supportive roles, others play the trigger, but all are participating in our growth. The question is: are we paying attention?

Our bodies are vessels—divinely chosen templates to support the lessons our soul agreed to learn in this lifetime. Some are here to explore physical strength, others to understand the intricacies of science or express the beauty of creation through art. Some souls incarnate as teachers, healers, guides, or disruptors, but all are here to help us remember. Help us to realign to the truth of who we really are.

Perhaps your boss denies you the raise you desire. Rather than blaming outwardly, consider how you may be feeling internally. Is there a part of you that does agree with your boss on an unconscious level that yes, in fact, you do feel unworthy of this raise? Are you resisting abundance because you fear the responsibility of having to handle larger sums of money? When we observe and release the internal belief systems which no longer align to our consciousness, we no longer need the repetition of the lessons of unworthiness or lack of abundance. However, if we avoid the insight and lean towards external validation, the pattern will return in other forms.

The people you walk through life with—yes, even the ones who hurt you—agreed to help you be the highest version of yourself. Maybe you struggle to show up for others, and so others stop showing up for you. Maybe you don't trust yourself, and people mirror that lack of trust and give you reasons to continue the beliefs of not being able to trust. Maybe you undervalue your worth, and so others take advantage of you. These experiences are invitations for deeper awareness and, ultimately, for healing–not only healing yourself, but also healing the generations that came before and will come after you.

Remember we are all here to remember and know who we are. We may take different paths during our search of knowing, yet the destination will always remain the same. Every soul yearns to return home, the return to the knowing of oneness with God.

God & Energy

The law of conservation states that energy cannot be created or destroyed, only transformed. This truth echoes the nature of the soul... and of God. God was not created, cannot be destroyed, and is ever-transforming.

Energy manifests in many forms: mechanical, thermal, nuclear, chemical, electromagnetic, sonic, gravitational, kinetic, and more. Light is electromagnetic energy. Sound—our words—is sonic energy. Even thoughts and emotions, often overlooked, are powerful energetic forces. Energy vibrates at different rates; this is known as frequency.

Each one of our thoughts is a frequency which, when emitted, reverberates through the entire universe and beyond. When you think of something with enough belief, intentional energy, and inspired action you begin to magnetize it into forming into your reality.

For example, if the collective truly believed the sky was purple, the sky would then change into the color purple—because the collective belief will direct the energy to transform the sky. If enough people observe or tune into a certain program, belief, intention, or frequency, it will manifest, which is also why there is always such a pull to control what is seen across certain platforms. It is no surprise that when you turn on the news for example, that you are subjected to a multitude of fear based programs. Keeping viewers in a fear based state or in a state of fight or flight in turn siphons energy and catalyzes people to react based on their fear and trauma or fight or flight responses. Therefore the collective energy overlay is that of a heavy trauma or fear based energetic pattern, which catalyzes world events towards that trajectory.

Emotion is energy in motion. It is neutral at its core but becomes charged based on how we label it, or the judgment we place upon it. Authenticity and love vibrate at higher frequencies/faster. Fear, anger, and guilt at lower frequencies/slower. Your emotional state of being, or frequency, will attract/magnetize people and experiences to validate this. Begin your day with gratitude, and more reasons to feel grateful will find you. Begin your day with a fear based program and more fear will follow.

Words are not just merely sounds—they are sonic waves that shape reality. Words bring form to the formless, they set the intention for the infinite to manifest. "...God said, 'Let there be light.'" Speaking with love and intention anchors unity and creation into what it is you are speaking of. Speaking with judgment or distortion echoes separation back into your own field of reality and the reality of those you are speaking of. Remember, you are always creating with your voice, even when you choose *not* to speak.

Your action or will are energy in motion. Each choice you make navigates the trajectory of your experience AKA your reality. Even making what we would consider to be a very small decision—like taking a different route home—could align you with unexpected blessings. However, repeating the same actions day after day without change often leads to stagnation, with the same experiences circling around waiting for us to observe said pattern or cycle.

Your action or will are represented by your intention. Intention is the force that directs the movement of energy. Intention gives shape to your thoughts, power to your words, direction to your emotions, and weight to your actions. If your intentions are rooted in love, you will manifest more reasons for love. If they are rooted in fear or lack, then that too will manifest.

Remember: Like Attracts Like. You are not separate from God. You are an extension, a conscious living reflection. And just like God, you are able to shape reality.

The Body and Soul Lesson Connection

Our bodies are brilliant creations of God. Our bodies were made in His image. Intelligently designed, extremely sophisticated and able to project our most sacred aspect: the soul. When a baby begins to form in the womb, the first internal system to develop is the nervous system—a network of energy pathways that sends signals to the brain to initiate action. It is no coincidence that this energetic system forms first, it's as if it's a reminder of our truest nature, infinite source energy manifesting in physical form.

Our body utilizes energy. Almost every cell in the body contains mitochondria, which generate ATP—our cellular energy source. This is the power that sustains life for most cells, and it is yet another example of the divine energy of God sustaining life in all living things. Plants, animals, and even fungi share this energetic structure. All life, at its core essence, is activated by God.

Our physical forms, our bodies, vary in shape, size, and color. Some are tall, some small, some dark, some light. Some are born with minds that create intellectually, others with bodies that create artistically. Our bodies are but one reflection of the tangible brilliance of God.

The very elements that form our physical bodies are the same elements found in planets, stars, and galaxies, which mirrors our infinite nature. Our soul is a reflection of the consciousness of God—eternal, radiant, and life-giving. Just as the sun sustains life by radiating energy, so too does the soul animate and give life to the body. If the sun were to extinguish, all life on Earth would cease to exist. In the same respect, when our soul leaves this body, the body ceases to function. The phrase "you are the son/sun of God" embodies the divine truth that you are a reflection or mirror of God. If we are the light of God, why on earth did we decide to experience bodies?

God created our bodies so we could experience life at one of the densest levels of creation. Each one of us has agreed to play a role for one another in this life. Each role we play is an example of a different level of expression tied to belief systems, emotions, thought projections and the current level of our consciousness. Our bodies are akin to a costume which we have assigned to ourselves to assist our soul's growth and expansion.

Just as different actors wear different costumes to help differentiate who they are or represent in movies and shows, we too experience life through different bodies. Let me ask you this: if you were watching a movie and everyone was wearing the same costume, wouldn't you figure out who the movie was really about well before anyone even uttered a word?

While we may obsess over our appearance or our lack of certain physical traits, few come to understand or accept that we chose our bodies purposefully prior to incarnation.

Before birth, we selected the shape, size, color, and talents that would best serve our soul's growth. We even set up parameters for our bodies to experience certain events depending on our emotional/mental states simply to bring attention to the discordant thought or emotional patterns. All of these decisions were made with divine precision, which you can have access to as long as you allow yourself to view it all from a higher level of consciousness or level of awareness.

For example, you could have judged someone with a physical disability in a previous incarnation or past life, and so in this life, you may experience a physical disability of some kind to help expand your consciousness surrounding disabilities. Maybe you relied heavily on your beauty to control the outcomes of situations or to control others in a previous life, so in this life, your soul may choose a more modest appearance to develop your intellect or creativity. Perhaps you starved in a past incarnation, and now you struggle with overeating or under-eating. Or maybe you were a warrior who needed strength and stamina, and now you're an athlete drawn to discipline and physical power.

In other cases, your soul might be learning resilience and surrender, and so you chose a body that would experience illness or limitation—calling forth your inner strength, your faith, and your capacity to overcome. Every detail of your body has been chosen to serve your higher evolution.

Honor your body. Your body is your temple. Thank your soul for your body. This body you occupy is not random—it is your greatest teacher, supporting your growth on all levels: physically, mentally, emotionally, and spiritually, as long as you allow it to do so.

I invite you now to allow yourself to see your body from this higher perspective. If you are not sure where to begin, this simple prayer is an easy guide:

"Holy Spirit, Father-Mother God of the Highest Source, I don't know the purpose of my body and I don't know what my body is supposed to teach me, but I am willing to learn."

Allow yourself the time and space to receive any insights that come on the lines provided below. Have faith and allow yourself to receive the insights in the way you learn best. God knows exactly how to deliver a message to you, loud and clear.

Take a deep breath, recite the prayer above if needed, and allow yourself to write the insights you receive below:

_____

_____

_____

Dis-ease and Pain: Divine Messages in Form

Have you ever wondered why some people are constantly afflicted by pain or dis-ease, while others seem to move through life untouched by physical suffering? Have you ever asked what triggers the onset of illness or why healing feels elusive for some? Did you notice that I wrote, dis-ease rather than disease—that's intentional. Dis-ease helps to reframe the way we relate to illness, shifting the perception from victimhood to empowerment. Words carry vibration and by hyphenating the word, it allows you to slow down and key in on any hidden insight.

Dis-Ease | Dis-Harmony | Non Harmonious | No Balance

Pain and dis-ease are your body's way of signaling an imbalance, this imbalance may stem from a physical, mental, emotional, or spiritual origin. Pain and dis-ease is not meaningless, it is the soul's call for attention through the language the physical form knows—sensation, restriction, and pain. Our bodies are divine messengers, perfectly designed to communicate what our minds may deny or what our hearts may suppress.

When we're healthy, we tend to ignore our body. Then, when pain arises or dis-ease takes root, we suddenly become acutely aware of our habits, our thoughts, our emotions, and even our current life path. Pain brings presence.

Western culture has taught us to numb the symptoms: take a pill, power through, find a quick fix. Headache? Take some medication. Anxiety or depression? Here's a prescription. Low energy? Drink some caffeine. Weight concerns? Here's something that drops your weight but you could also die in the process.

While some medications are absolutely life-saving and necessary in acute cases, many of our day-to-day imbalances are not meant to be masked—they're meant to be met.

These symptoms are sacred clues to what lies beneath the surface. Have you ever had a gut feeling that warned you about something? When you listened, you were protected. When you ignored it, you learned why you should have paid attention. That intuitive nudge is your soul speaking through your body. Our body is an instrument of divine intelligence. What if your back pain wasn't just about poor posture but actually about the financial burdens you've been carrying? What if your chronic illness wasn't a punishment but a portal to deeper understanding of the wounds you're unconsciously carrying, or have consciously stuffed away?

When we experience emotional trauma—big or small—our body quite literally stores it. Think of your body as a giant computer, capable of downloading different programs into its system. These programs can be activated to run depending on the type of mental, emotional, physical, or energetic trigger. These programs can also be modified or changed depending on your willingness to resolve them. The body will hold or store these programs in many places, one of which being the fascia; the connective tissue that holds our entire physical form together. Fascia can be understood as a crystalline matrix, capable of recording memories from the time of conception. It remembers joy, love, grief, fear, and everything in between. Think of your fascia as the stuff that holds it all together so you're not just a giant meat suit blob sloshing around all day.

Now, let's say you touched a flame as a child, the pain you felt while touching the flame created an imprint of information from this experience into your fascia. This imprint is then stored in the fascia of your thumb or anywhere else in your body. The heat sensation caused by the flame has signaled fight or flight response, thus causing the activation of your parasympathetic nervous system. Your reaction is to pull away from the flame, and an energetic signature is imprinted into your fascia as a way to protect you from touching a flame again. Make sense?

Now, imagine every single experience you have ever had, since birth. Kind of hard to think of it all, right? Well, you actually never forgot any of it. Your body remembers it all and stores it for you until you are ready to unpack it.

Sometimes we start to unpack it consciously but mostly it recycles unconsciously through multiple feedback loops or trauma responses. Not only does our fascia record physical events, it also stores all of our emotional burns of heartbreak, loss, abandonment, grief, or shame. These physical, mental, emotional, and energetic imprints eventually become energetic blockages. When these blockages or imbalances are left unresolved, they will manifest in physical form as pain or dis-ease.

Pain and dis-ease are not here to punish you—they are here to awaken you. It is an opportunity to slow down, to listen deeply, and to heal something buried within. When we take time to sit with the pain, feel into it, ask what it's trying to say, then act on that wisdom, we allow healing to begin. Once the emotional root is acknowledged and integrated, the physical symptoms no longer need to persist, they simply fall away.

Let this truth settle in: your body is not betraying you. It is working for you always, doing its best to help you awaken, evolve, and return to wholeness.

Body Connection: Mediation and Journaling

Read through fully before attempting, this helps maintain the
flow of energy

Allow yourself to sit comfortably with your feet on the ground
and your hands resting on your legs, palms up.

Bring your attention to your heart, and imagine the more you
focus, the more you feel a swirling sensation in and around your chest.

Allow yourself to focus on your heart energy, and allow yourself
to feel it building.

Say internally or out loud:

"Divine Holy Spirit, Father-Mother God, I don't know what my
body wants to tell me about "................", but I am willing to
surrender my body to you so that I may learn."

Now take a deep breath all the way to your toes, hold for 3
seconds and allow yourself to fully breathe out all doubt.

Allow yourself to take another deep breath in, hold for 4 seconds,
then allow yourself to fully breathe out all fear.

On this final breath in, allow yourself to see yourself breathing in
golden white light, and hold for 3 seconds. This time as you breathe
out, visualize yourself blowing out golden white light within and

around your entire body. As it engulfs your body, you begin to feel cradled in a womb of white and gold light.

With your imagination, allow yourself to see yourself standing in front of your body.

Say, "I allow myself to see what God wants to show me"

You may start to receive feelings/emotions that your body is ready to release, this may appear as burps, coughing, or tears. You may receive insights as actual words–thought patterns or belief systems that are ready to be released–you may also be shown past people/events that need forgiveness. Whatever comes through, trust and know that you are ready to release it and it is for your highest good.

Allow yourself some time to write the messages you receive below:

_____

_____

_____

_____

_____

_____

_____

Emotional Alchemy: De-Coding the Body

When de-coding/de-constructing the messages behind pain or dis-ease in the body, it's essential to view it both literally and symbolically. This is the sacred dialogue between logic and creativity/intuition—the left and right hemispheres of your brain working in harmony to reveal higher perspectives and deeper insight to the foundations of your life.

The physical location of pain in your body can hold literal meaning. The emotion(s) attached to it, often manifest as symbolic and points to something much deeper. Your body speaks in metaphor, and the soul uses your body as a canvas to relay divine insight.

One powerful lens of interpretation lies in recognizing the duality within the body. The left side corresponds with feminine energy—receptivity, intuition, and the divine mother. The right side corresponds with masculine energy—action, structure, and the divine father. When pain arises on a specific side, it ultimately relates to a wound associated with your relationship to either the feminine or masculine energies of God. I know this may be hard to understand, but everything leads back to God. Uncovering your wounds between you and God usually happens towards the end stages of kundalini activations and ascension cycles. Not to say that once those wounds start to be worked through that there won't be more activations and ascension cycles because there will be until your soul is ready to return to the absolute bliss state of be-ing of One-ness, complete unity with the infinite. Until that happens, our consciousness and belief systems, wounds and triggers will be reflected back to us through multiple outlets and avenues, one of which is your body.

Here are some common areas of the body and the emotional/spiritual symbolism they may hold. Keep in mind, these are not universal truths - meaning they may vary from person to person. The information that I am sharing has been given to me during sessions with clients. I have decided to include this so that they can be powerful starting points for your self-inquiry. Your soul knows what resonates.

I.   Eyes

Something we refuse to see. Are you unwilling to look at a truth or an event in your life? The left eye may point to a feminine influence or divine mother wound. The right eye may signal a male influence or divine father wound. Needing to see it in order to believe it, refusing to accept that there is nothing outside of what is physically seen. Not allowing oneself to see the bigger picture. Not wanting to see things from a different perspective. Being blinded by the truth.

II.   Ears

Something you do not want to hear. Is there truth being spoken around you—or within you—that you are blocking out or refusing to listen to? Stubborn, in one ear out the other. Unable to take criticism, not willing to listen to other perspectives. Not enough balance between what is being expressed and what is being retained.

III.   Jaw

Unspoken words or suppressed truth. Are you holding back your voice out of fear or shame? Are you biting your tongue to keep the peace? Afraid to rock the boat, people-pleasing tendencies. Could have been killed in a past life for speaking out. Could have been persecuted for telling the truth. Childhood trauma of being told not to speak, not to talk back, being made fun of in school for speaking or reading out loud. Believing that one does not have any authority to speak on anything.

IV.   Neck

Someone could quite literally be a pain in your neck—mental or emotional rigidity—an unwillingness to see a different perspective. Our neck allows our head to turn towards different opportunities or environments. Past life trauma or death incident. The stress of keeping your head up while carrying many burdens. Not allowing oneself to see the bigger picture. Carrying unprocessed emotional wounds or trauma.

V.   Throat

A shutdown of self-expression, a suppression of speaking out, speaking your truth, or a fear that your voice is not worthy of being heard. Being forced to speak things that do not align with how you honestly feel. Past life trauma or death injury: drowning, strangulation, hanging, decapitation. The throat chakra is your communication center.

VI.   Shoulders

We carry the weight of the world on our shoulders or Atlas–our internal and external world. This area holds emotional and mental burdens, stress, and the pain we absorb from others when we carry what is not ours. Left–feminine or mother wounds or divine mother. Right–masculine or father, or divine father wounds. When people unload their day or an event onto us, we can absorb their burdens into our shoulders and traps instead of observing and assigning an angel to help them. (I bet you didn't think you could assign an angel to someone to help them, well I am here to inform you that you absolutely can!)

VII.   Elbows

Symbolic of support and flexibility. Elbow pain may indicate a feeling of not being supported or an unwillingness to bend to life's changes. Left side–not feeling supported in relationships with females and ultimately the divine mother. Right side–not feeling supported in relationships with males and ultimately the divine father. Not willing to be flexible to help others. Having too many boundaries which incapacitates beliefs around not being worthy of being supported.

VIII.   Wrists

Wrists provide directional movement for our hands; wrists help our hands shift things around. Resistant to shifts, resistance to letting go. Are you holding on too tightly to a situation, belief, or person out of fear. Are you afraid of energy shifting around you, does that make you feel out of control? Energetic or emotional barriers around releasing or receiving.

IX.   Hands

Our ability to hold, receive, give, and let go, also an extension of your heart. Pain in the hands can reflect clinging to what no longer serves you or feeling unable to give or receive freely. The left hand (feminine) can represent receiving. The right hand (masculine) can represent giving. Pain in your hands could also be triggered by a healer blocking their own healing abilities because of their foundational belief programs or patterns being in discordance with disbelief of the ability for humans to heal themselves.

X.   Chest/Heart

Can reflect deep emotional pain, grief, or heartbreak. Traumatic loss, deaths, or experiences related to loved ones can be stored in this area. Pain can also arise if you are not following your heart, or if you have closed your heart out of fear of being hurt or as a trauma response. Hardened Heart, being forced not to show emotions as a child or adult. Feeling unloved, unlovable, or unnurtured. Left side = feminine wounds. Right side = masculine wounds.

XI.   Abdomen

Powerlessness, believing one has no power. Victim mentality, victimhood consciousness. Depression–losing your spark or feeling completely out of control of what's happening in life. This area represents your will, your drive, your personal power, and your ability to make decisions. Who are you blaming or projecting onto? Feeling fragmented, feeling like everyone is out to get you, paranoid. Fear of the future and fear of the unknown. Past life wounding or tragic death being activated during the same age timeframe as past life to be cleared.

Digestive issues often symbolize an inability to 'stomach' something in life. Suppressed creativity, constant anxiety, or emotional turmoil often reside here.

XII.   Hips

Hips help your legs pivot and provide directional movement. Are you suffering with indecision or does it feel like you're stuck at a crossroad? A powerful client story illustrates this: after seven years of unresolved hip pain, countless MRIs, doctors, and injections, I helped a client realize the root cause of his hip pain was his refusal to decide whether or not to retire. Once he committed to a decision, his hip pain completely released! Feeling unsure of making a decision. Not trusting in one's ability to make a decision. Being stuck in fight or flight for long periods of time around a decision.

XIII.   Legs

Symbolize a mental, emotional or physical block or fear of moving forward. Are you hesitating to take the next step in life? Are you living too much in the future, frozen in fear? Or are you so focused on the past that you feel stuck? Your legs can also represent your fear of taking the wrong step or the annoyance of having to back track and retrace your steps. Restless legs are triggered from anxiety being stored in the legs and unable to be grounded or released.

XIV.   Knees

The knees help us bend our legs, which also helps us to jump or take leaps of faith. Our knees are also correlated to our ego. Pain or discomfort here can reflect wounded pride, ruminating thoughts about other people that you tend to keep to yourself, stubbornness, or the need to protect oneself internally or externally. Inner knee–internal world, your internal belief systems/programs may cause you to fear certain people/situations/ lose personal relationships. Outer knee– external influences, traumatic outward experiences in this life or past lives where the focus is on more external projections rather than inward.

XV.   Feet

Your feet represent your foundation—things such as your foundational experiences, traits/beliefs/patterns/programs passed on from generation to generation. Our feet help us with grounding and releasing, as well as receiving new information from the earth and your surroundings. Are you holding onto outdated programming or belief systems that keep you from moving freely? Plantar Fasciitis usually occurs when a person is unable to release or shift their foundational belief systems or programs, this can happen when they are being introduced to new information which goes against everything they were either raised to believe or came into believing as their truth during the course of their lives.

XVI.   Back

The back can reflect the hidden burdens we are carrying, since the back encompasses many chakras, there can be multiple types of distortions:

• Upper back (Heart Chakra): Grief, heartbreak, emotional betrayal, getting backstabbed. Judgements we've placed on ourselves and others.

• Mid back (Solar Plexus): Loss of power, giving power away, feeling like you are under too much pressure from yourself or others to perform.

• Between mid and lower (Sacral): Suppressed creativity or self-worth. Ancestral Trauma. Feeling unworthy to create. Generational burdens.

• Lower back/Sciatic (Root Chakra): Security issues, sexual abuse, financial stress, relationship imbalances- internal and external, not wanting to be in your body, not feeling safe in your body.

These energetic patterns are invitations—not diagnoses. They are whispers from your soul, asking you to pay attention, and to seek deeper. When you listen with love, the body doesn't need to scream. When you heal the emotional root, the physical pain can dissolve. This is emotional alchemy.

I have provided a few open lines of pages to help you identify what it is your body may be trying to tell you. If you are unsure of what might be coming through, or if you would like some higher assistance, I suggest saying this prayer after you have identified the pain/dis-ease:

"Divine Holy Spirit, Father-Mother God of the Highest Consciousness, I don't know what my body is trying to tell me with "..........", but I am willing surrender all I know and all I don't know to learn."

Do your best not to doubt, judge, or minimize what wants to be written, just allow it to be written. You will find the more you do these exercises the deeper you are able to go and more connections will start to surface. You may have to repeat the prayer a few times depending on how willing you are to surrender the identity you have attached to said pain or disease. You may find there are certain people or events that need to be forgiven through this exercise as well, do your best to do so with grace and love, for yourself and all involved.

Pain / Disease Location:_____ Left or Right Side:_____

Message or Meaning:

_____

_____

_____

_____

_____

_____

_____

_____

_____

Pain / Disease Location:_____ Left or Right Side:_____

Message or Meaning:

_____

_____

_____

_____

_____

_____

_____

_____

_____

Pain / Disease Location:_____ Left
or Right Side:_____

Message or Meaning:

_____

_____

_____

_____

_____

_____

_____

_____

_____

Pain / Disease Location:_____ Left
or Right Side:_____

Message or Meaning:

_____

_____

_____

_____

_____

_____

_____

_____

_____

_____

Pain / Disease Location:_____ Left or Right Side:_____

Message or Meaning:

_____

_____

_____

_____

_____

_____

_____

_____

Pain / Disease Location:_____ Left or Right Side:_____

Message or Meaning:

_____

_____

Perception and Judgment: Mirrors of Consciousness

Every day, we witness how our experiences are filtered through our perception and, often, we don't realize we are wearing a lens at all.

Reality isn't as objective as we like to think. It is shaped by the beliefs we carry—many of which we never consciously chose. They come from childhood, ancestral memory, past lives, or the energetic imprint overlays of the collective or of this current incarnation. These beliefs create internal programs and those programs become the lenses through which we judge the world and our place in it.

Judgment, in its rawest form, is simply comparison born from perception.

It doesn't matter whether a belief was formed in childhood or last week. What matters is whether we're willing to bring awareness to it now. To ask ourselves: is this still true for me? Is this expanding me or limiting me? Am I giving value to something that is now valueless to me?

Most people do not take the time to ask themselves these questions. They move through life assuming that everything happening around them is random, unfair, or externally driven. This is the root of what many call victim consciousness. It detaches responsibility, and with it, it also dissolves personal power.

Understand that we are always being invited to understand or see things from a higher perspective, and this leads us to explore one of my dreams.

Spirit's Spotlight: "School and the Glasses"

I found myself walking through a school with a group of people. I felt connected to their souls. I didn't recognize the people in the group, but they all felt familiar as if we had all been here together before. There was one woman leading us, and, even though I didn't recognize her from this life, I knew her deeply. She wore a light blue headdress, similar to what Mother Mary might wear—soft, elegant, and draped just below her shoulders. Her energy was kind, grounded, compassionate, and clear. I knew I trusted her completely, and I was more than elated to be exploring this school with her.

We moved from room to room, taking inventory of what belonged and what no longer served us. We were searching for things within the school that we could either get rid of or change—books, chalkboards, pens, desks. These are symbols of learning, of knowledge, of the tools we use to make sense of our soul's experience on Earth. It felt like we were rearranging everything, realigning the lessons with divine order. The process felt chaotic at times because everything was thrown everywhere and there was no sense of direction. We just knew what we had to do so we kept searching through the school.

What stood out to me most was the pair of glasses I was wearing. I do not wear glasses in my waking state, so I hadn't realized they were on me until I tried to navigate through a huge pile of books. At one point I bumped into a pile of books, this was when I realized I was even wearing glasses to begin with. Whenever the glasses would shift or move even just slightly, my vision would blur and sometimes split right down the middle.

I didn't think anything of it, I just kept moving and adjusting them whenever they would start to fall. At one point, I turned to show the female guide what I had found, but when I turned the glasses fell completely off my eyes. It was at that moment that everything disappeared! I couldn't see anything, but it wasn't a black void, it was just a pure white room.

I stood there frozen for a moment, wondering what the heck had just happened. I felt the glasses resting just below my nose so I adjusted them back onto my face and bam! Everyone was back as if nothing had changed. The room was still there, the school was still there. All the people I was working alongside were still going around gathering items, and the female guide was still, in fact, guiding.

With a smile on my face, I turned towards the guide and said, "You know, there's something you're not telling me about these glasses." The guide just looked at me with a smile on her face, so I continued, "When my glasses fall off, I can't see you, I can't see anything except me, everything disappears and it's just me that's left.

So there's something you're definitely not telling me about these lenses."

It was at that moment that everyone in the group, including the guide, started giggling joyfully. It was as if they knew all along, and I found myself awakening to the sacred giggles.

That dream was a metaphor for how our reality changes based on our levels of perception/consciousness. The glasses represented my filters, my lenses of perception, the stories and beliefs that color everything I see. When they were on, I could see the separation between myself and everyone else around me. When the glasses or lenses shifted, everyone disappeared and I was the only one left. This represents how we see many things as separate from ourselves, when in reality they are simply mirrors to us all.

The words I spoke still echoed in my heart upon awakening, "There's something you're not telling me about these lenses." It was an invitation to become conscious of my filters, of the lenses of perception that I am projecting onto myself and others. To examine what I might be avoiding or distorting. It was a gentle nudge to explore the unconscious stories still shaping how I see others, myself, and even God.

Choosing a Higher Lens

We always have a choice in how we perceive or receive information from people, places, and events in life. We have the option to look at life through the lens of fear and judgment or through the lens of love and wholeness. The higher the lens, the deeper the truth.

When we pause to observe without judgment, when we allow ourselves to be curious about emotional patterns or mental loops, we reclaim our power. It doesn't mean we bypass pain. It means we sit with it long enough to understand it, not to attach more stories to, but to understand where those stories came from. This really allows us to start to forgive through deeper levels of awareness.

First, I had to forgive myself for believing I needed to wear certain lenses to stay safe. For seeing through filters that were inherited or born from trauma. I forgave myself for every moment I judged someone else without realizing they were reflecting something I hadn't yet healed within me.

With each layer of forgiveness, I felt the lenses begin to shift. They became clearer. Lighter. Less distorting.

Just like in my dream, when the glasses shifted, I could see again. Not just my immediate surroundings, but the purpose, the guidance, the presence of those walking with me. I could see the sacredness of the school, the divine orchestration of the lessons, and the eternal presence of the guide, God.

The purpose is not to discard our lenses or perceptions, it's about becoming conscious of them, adjusting them, undistorting them and, most of all, remembering that when we look through the "lense of God," we no longer view ourselves as separate, but instead as an integral part of all that is.

Healing the Separation from God

Jesus said, "Those who seek should not stop seeking until they find. When they find it, they will be disturbed. When they are disturbed, they will marvel—and will reign over all."

That teaching sparked something within me. It echoed louder and louder as I stepped deeper into my healing, into the places within me I once avoided. And when I got quiet—truly quiet—I began to see that the core issue behind every wound, every loop, every program I've ever tried to clear… wasn't just about another person. It was about my relationship with God.

At first, this was hard to grasp. I had always seen abandonment, betrayal, or mistrust as things that other people had done to me. The more I surrendered my healing to God and the Holy Spirit, the more I began to understand:

Every unresolved wound I carried was a distortion or wound between me and God.

Core Wounds

The fear of abandonment or lack of worthiness doesn't start with a parent, a partner, or a past life connection. It started the moment our souls believed we were separate from God. We wondered what it would be like to be on our own—to experience contrast, polarity, and individual will. That desire to explore birthed the veil of separation.

With each incarnation, that veil thickened. The memory of oneness faded. And instead, we gathered experiences of betrayal, abandonment, judgment, rejection—layer upon layer—all reflecting that first illusion: I am not one with God.

But that illusion became painful. We started to believe that God had left us, that we were unworthy, that love was something to earn, that safety had to be fought for. Each of these beliefs fragmented the soul further. Until we were buried beneath shame, rage, fear, despair, and unworthiness.

Yet, something miraculous happens when we trace our wounds all the way back to its root—when we arrive at that core fracture between us and God. Once we perceive it, or become conscious of it, we can release it. When we release it, we don't just heal ourselves—we free every version of ourselves, in every timeline, who carried that same distortion/wound. Just like dominos, as our core wounds fall away, the mental/emotional/physical distortions around those wounds dissolve too.

To have a greater understanding of any core wounds you are ready to release, let us take the time now to surrender all that we are ready to surrender to help us uncover this truth.

"Divine Holy Spirit, Father-Mother God, I don't know what core wounds I may be holding against you, but I am willing to learn and surrender all my wounds to you now. I allow myself to forgive any wounds that I am carrying towards you God."

Allow yourself the space to write and release all that would like to come through you now:

_____

_____

_____

_____

_____

_____

_____

_____

_____

The Path of Forgiveness

Once I started to identify the core wounds, I began by forgiving myself for even thinking I could be separate from God.

For believing that God would abandon me.

For thinking that God would judge me.

For fearing God.

For being angry at God for "letting it happen."

For believing I was unworthy of being loved by God.

And most of all—for believing that God didn't love me.

This process was not easy. It disturbed me, just like Jesus said it would. It brought tears, trembling, and waves of grief that felt like they came from lifetimes I had forgotten. But, through the sorrow came something else: relief.

Because each time I forgave myself, I felt the veil of separation and illusion begin to lift. Each time I forgave I allowed different pathways of expression to be released, clearing, cleaning, and redefining how I viewed God as well as myself.

My Core Wound: Trust

"You just gotta trust. That's the final boss, it's the hardest to beat." That was a download I received one evening while playing Fortnite. Immediately, my stomach sank. Does this mean I'm going to be physically and emotionally tested again on trust?

I, like many souls, have been lied to, cheated on, manipulated, and taken advantage of physically, mentally, emotionally, and even spiritually. I have had every reason not to trust people, I was sexually assaulted at a young age, tortured by entities, backstabbed and bruised by humans, made to feel dirty and unworthy. In theory, I could sit down with anyone and explain why I don't trust based on my past experiences, and they would most likely agree that my distrust is justified, especially when it involves being taken advantage of as a child.

I understand that everything is a reflection of me, so how can I view my core wound of trust through this level of consciousness or awareness?

And then I could finally see. I marveled at it, just as that quote said I would.

I marveled at how intricately my core wound wove into each experience around trust. My distrust in people had been a mirror of my distrust in God.

I didn't trust that God would keep me safe.

I didn't trust that God would protect me.

I didn't trust that God would provide for me.

I didn't trust that God would guide me.

I didn't trust that God would choose me, hear me, love me, or stay with me.

I wept. Not out of pain, but because recognizing those wounds felt like liberation. Multiple burdens lifted. The tears shifted then to immense tears of joy, pouring out of every ounce of my being. For the first time in my life I finally felt closer to home.

The Final Boss

When I heard the words, "You just gotta trust. That's the final boss, it's the hardest to beat," my initial thought was this boss to be defeated was something or someone outside of myself. In reality, it was inside of me the entire time. The final boss was the ego's multiple illusions: fear, separation, unworthiness, and mistrust.

Those illusions took many forms in current and previous relationships. They all simply mirrored my wounded beliefs between me and God. Past relationships, people, and situations were never the problem, they were simply the reflection.

To further this healing, I began journaling every trauma I could remember. Starting with childhood, I went as far back as I could remember, all the way back to Jersey City. I also asked God to help me to see anything and remember anything that I couldn't. I looked at the core emotions and thought patterns beneath abandonment, jealousy, fear, anger, shame, resentment, and distrust.

Then I rewrote the stories.

I imagined each situation and what it would look like from a higher perspective. Between me and God.

Instead of viewing my experiences from the emotions and projections between myself and others, I rewrote the stories from a perspective of projections between me and God. Every other person involved in my story was now God.

How can this shift of perspective change the way you perceive your life thus far?

It was uncomfortable and also kind of weird at first, but extremely eye-opening. I found that my issues with God were simply being reflected back to me through each person who had "hurt me." They were simply mirroring the pain and trauma I was carrying forth from lifetime to lifetime, as well as the trauma we are collectively born into.

This may be a point in your journey where you start doing intense shadow work, even the name of it implies something dark and scary. Shadow work is nothing to fear, it's simply something that you have not brought to the light.. A lower level of awareness, something you are yet to be made aware of.

Even though you may not be aware of your shadow, know that it has the ability to ascend into higher levels of awareness or consciousness. Thus helping you achieve higher states of awareness once observed. Therefore, shadow work is simply a tool to highlight areas where you can add higher levels of awareness to your consciousness. That being said, if we do the shadow work on our core wounds, we then allow ourselves to be free from those lower levels of awareness, consciousness, overlays or energetic vibrations.

In order for one to be made aware of their shadow, you must allow yourself to see it. Once you allow yourself to see it, you then allow yourself to change or transmute it. As you allow the change and transmutation to anchor within yourself, you then anchor the change into the reality you experience. While at the same time freeing those you have attached to your wounds. Which then expands upon the healing the collective is able to participate in. As above, so below – as within, so without.

I would like to share a prayer for forgiveness I wrote after I received this download:

I forgive all souls who have mirrored my wounds, for they were simply playing their part in showing my soul where I am still holding to beliefs that no longer serve my consciousness. Most importantly, I forgive my soul for believing in these projections. I forgive my soul for believing God doesn't love me. I forgive my soul for believing God wouldn't guide me. I forgive my soul for believing God wouldn't choose me. I forgive my soul

101

for believing God wouldn't protect me. I forgive my soul for believing that God is not with me. I forgive my soul for believing I couldn't hear God. I forgive my soul for believing I wasn't worthy of God.. I forgive my soul for believing God doesn't remember me. I forgive my soul for believing God would leave me behind.

I forgive myself and allow God to help me transmute this.. And in doing so… I return home.

A Conversation with God: Your Invitation Inward

As you read those words, perhaps something inside you started to stir. Maybe memories are rising. Maybe tears are forming. Maybe your heart is whispering, "This is what I've been carrying, too."

If that's true—then I invite you now into the most sacred space there is: the space within your own heart, where the living God dwells.

Take a breath. Say this prayer with surrender:

"Divine Holy Spirit, Father-Mother God, I don't know what wounds I carry against you but I am willing to forgive them, forgive you and forgive myself too."

Say it as many times as you need until your soul begins to soften. Then, take a breath and listen.

You may not hear words. You may feel warmth, see color, or receive a subtle shift. Or you may feel nothing at all—yet. But trust this: something sacred just happened, and you became more willing to heal.

These next few pages are for you—just you and God. Use it to write what you hear, what you feel, or simply what you've been needing to say to God.

Your Conversation with God

Chakras: A Divine Design

Chakras are not just spinning wheels of energy, they are access points to portals of consciousness encoded with the divine intelligence of your soul's journey through form. These vortexes are multidimensional interface points between your physical body, emotional field, mental matrix, and soul light. They give and receive energy, but they also store memory, access timelines, activate latent gifts, and bridge your connection to God.

While many know of the seven chakras along the spine, this is only the beginning. These seven gateways are mirrors of a much larger system—like keys on a piano that can play a symphony of higher dimensional awareness.

Each chakra governs a layer of your human experience, while also acting as a portal to your spiritual evolution. When aligned and balanced, they allow energy to flow freely between you and Source. When stagnant, distorted, or overactive, they create imbalances— physically, emotionally, and spiritually. But beyond balance, the chakras are also teachers, revealing exactly where we are in our sacred remembering.

Let us now traverse through each of these sacred gateways—not only as energy centers, but as living wisdom keepers of your divine blueprint.

I.   Root Chakra: "I Am the Grounded Presence of God"

Location: base of the spine, pelvic floor, and legs

Color: red

Element: Earth

Associated glands/systems: adrenal glands, skeletal system, colon, legs, feet

The Root Chakra is more than your connection to survival—it is your divine right to exist in the physical realm. It is the anchoring point for your soul's incarnation on Earth, the place where you interface with gravity, time, and ancestral memory.

This chakra holds cellular memory from your ancestral bloodline—programs of survival, scarcity, displacement, war, land trauma, and tribal wounds. If your ancestors struggled to feel safe, were persecuted, or experienced generational poverty, these codes may still be running in your energetic field.

It also links you to Earth's crystalline grid, the network of ley lines and energy nodes that carry wisdom from ancient civilizations. When your Root is open and grounded, you plug into the Earth like a sacred extension of the Divine Mother. You feel held, stable, here.

Signs of imbalance:

Chronic fear or hypervigilance

Feeling unworthy of existence or embodiment

Hypo- or hyperactive sexual activity

Financial instability and survival anxiety

Disconnection from the body or fear of being "too human"

Floating, ungrounded energy, or escapism

Rage, inherited violence, or trauma-based aggression

Not wanting to be in your body

Sacred practices:

Stand barefoot on Earth and visualize roots growing into the crystalline grid

Eat grounding, mineral-rich foods (beets, root veggies, bone broth)

Connect with black tourmaline, ruby, hematite, or red jasper

Use drumming, walking meditation, or hip-based movement

Breathe into your pelvic bowl with the intention to anchor your soul

Yoni steaming practices

Advanced insight:

When activated, the Root Chakra begins to recode the DNA structure to release inherited karmic patterning and activate divine embodiment templates. This is the foundation of building the Lightbody on Earth.

Affirmations:

"I Am the Light of God Made Manifest."

"I Anchor Heaven Into Earth Through My Presence."

"My Body Is Sacred. My Existence Is Holy."

"I Am Supported, Protected, and Fully Alive."

"The Earth Remembers Me. I Belong Here."

II.   Sacral Chakra: "I Create Through the Divine Waters Within Me"

Location: lower abdomen, womb, and reproductive organs

Color: orange

Element: water

Associated glands/systems: reproductive system, bladder, kidneys, small intestine

The Sacral Chakra is the cosmic womb within you. It is where the spark of Source becomes form. Here, we create worlds through emotion, intimacy, play, and beauty. This is the seat of your sacred sexuality, divine creativity, and emotional fluidity.

Beyond art or procreation, the Sacral Chakra is where karmic contracts and Akashic memory are held. Sexual wounds, shame, betrayal, soul loss, and distortions of feminine/masculine energy are often stored here—not only from this life, but from many.

It also holds your capacity for pleasure and receptivity. Many who carry wounds from religious suppression, sexual trauma, or being forced to conform to inauthentic roles experience disconnection here.

Signs of imbalance:

Shame around sexuality or body

Inability to express or trust creativity

Emotional numbness or hypersensitivity

Relationship co-dependence or fear of intimacy

Guilt, repression, or excessive indulgence

Sacred practices:

Sacred sensual movement, belly dancing, or hip circles

Write poetry, paint, sing—creating for joy, not perfection

Water immersion (baths, oceans) with intention to release emotion

Work with carnelian, orange calcite, moonstone, or amber

Womb clearing or divine feminine/masculine balance meditations

Advanced insight:

This chakra holds the blueprint for divine union and divine conception. As you heal, you may begin to activate a higher octave of the sacral, where creation becomes sacred service and your energetic womb births timelines of collective healing.

Affirmations:

"I Am a Vessel of Sacred Creation."

"My Emotions Flow Freely and Safely."

"Pleasure Is My Birthright."

"I Release Shame and Embody Innocence."

"My Creations Serve the Highest Good of All."

III.   Solar Plexus Chakra: "I Embody the Will of the Divine"

Location: upper abdomen, between navel and sternum

Color: yellow

Element: fire

Associated glands/systems: pancreas, liver, stomach, metabolism

The Solar Plexus is the command center of your energy field. It governs willpower, confidence, self-trust, and boundaries. But on a deeper level, it houses your soul's mission codes—the blueprint of what you came to Earth to do.

When aligned, this chakra allows you to take courageous action in harmony with Divine Will. It dissolves fear of failure and the need for external validation. You lead not from ego, but from embodied spiritual authority.

When blocked, we feel powerless, invisible, anxious, or dominated by others. In hyperactive states, it manifests as control, overcompensation, or projection.

Signs of imbalance:

Self-doubt, anxiety, or paralysis

Over-assertiveness, competition, or control

People-pleasing or martyrdom

Digestive issues, adrenal burnout, emotional exhaustion

Feeling "off-purpose" or lost

Sacred practices:

Core-strengthening movement (yoga, breath of fire, martial arts)

Solar meditations—sit with the sun and breathe it into your belly

Journaling with the question what would I do if I trusted myself completely?

Work with citrine, pyrite, golden calcite, or sunstone

Declare healthy boundaries and act on intuitive "yes" or "no"

Advanced insight:

When the solar plexus activates at a higher octave, it becomes a beacon of solar light, broadcasting your divine resonance signature to the collective grid. This chakra transmits your frequency to call in aligned soul contracts and missions. The solar plexus starts to radiate a gold light when fully activated and aligned with God.

Affirmations:

"I Am a Sovereign Expression of Divine Will."

"My Power Is Safe, Holy, and Anchored in Love."

"I Trust My Inner Light to Guide Me."

"I Radiate Confidence, Purpose, and Truth."

"I Lead with Integrity and Grace."

"I Will To Be The Christ On Earth!"

IV.   Heart Chakra: "I Love As God Loves"

Location: center of the chest

Color: emerald green or soft rose

Element: air

Associated glands/systems: thymus gland, lungs, heart, circulatory system

The Heart Chakra is the center of the human-soul interface. It bridges the lower physical chakras with the upper spiritual chakras—merging the Earth and the Heavens within your chest. It governs not just love, but divine harmonic resonance—your capacity to live in balance, compassion, forgiveness, and higher truth.

But beyond emotion, the heart is a sacred portal. Its energy field is shaped like a torus, and when activated, it becomes a multidimensional gateway—often referred to as the seat of the Merkaba. It allows you to expand and contract through timelines, dimensions, and quantum realities while staying centered in unconditional love.

Trauma to the heart—loss, betrayal, rejection, grief—causes the field to contract or fragment. Many souls unconsciously close their heart field after suffering emotional wounds, limiting their ability to give and receive the love they deeply desire.

Signs of imbalance:

Isolation or fear of intimacy

Over-giving or martyr tendencies

Difficulty trusting or opening up emotionally

Resentment, grief, or loss of joy

Physical chest tension, heart palpitations, lung tightness

Sacred practices:

Heart coherence breathwork: inhale into the heart, exhale love

Practice self-forgiveness and inner child nurturing

Send silent blessings to others as well as yourself—"May you feel loved."

Use rose quartz, emerald, green aventurine, or rhodonite

Walk in nature with the intention of merging your heartbeat with the Earth

Advanced insight:

The heart is the first chakra that exists fully in multiple dimensions. It's the convergence point where timelines collapse, and soul fractals reunite. The more you clear your heart, the more your multidimensional Self and your gifts come online.

Affirmations:

"I Am a Beacon of Divine Love."

"Love Flows To Me, Through Me, As Me."

"My Heart Is Safe, Whole, and Expansive."

"I Forgive Myself and Others With Grace."

"I Anchor Heaven On Earth Through Compassion."

"I Allow The Living Waters of God to Flow Through Every Layer of Consciousness Within and Around My Heart."

V.   Throat Chakra: "I Speak the Frequency of Truth"

Location: throat, neck, jaw, and upper shoulders

Color: sky blue or aqua

Element: sound/ether

Associated glands/systems: thyroid, parathyroid, vocal cords, jaw, mouth

The Throat Chakra is more than your ability to speak—it is your timeline weaver. Words are spells. Vibration is creation. Every time you speak, you are commanding energy into motion. This chakra determines the frequency at which your reality crystallizes.

It is the bridge between thought and form—turning the unseen into the seen through frequency. When aligned, it empowers you to speak your truth with clarity, authenticity, and divine resonance. When blocked, it results in fear of judgment, self-censorship, or energetic shutdown.

Many carry soul wounds here from lifetimes where their voice was suppressed or persecuted—especially spiritual teachers, mystics, and spiritually gifted souls.

Signs of imbalance:

Fear of public speaking or voicing truth

Chronic throat issues, tight jaw, or neck tension

Passive-aggressiveness or explosive communication

Feeling unheard or unseen

Over-talking or withholding words altogether

Sacred practices:

Speak light codes or mantras aloud

Practice vocal toning and sound healing

Journal uncensored truths

Use aquamarine, blue kyanite, or lapis lazuli

Declare truth aloud: "I revoke all contracts that silence me."

Advanced insight:

The Throat Chakra is linked to the Akashic field. When fully opened, it allows you to access and rewrite your soul's destiny through conscious declaration. You become the living word, reauthoring your destiny in real time.

Affirmations:

"I Speak My Truth With Divine Clarity."

"My Voice Activates Healing and Alignment."

"I Express Myself Authentically and With Love."

"I Am Safe To Be Heard and Seen."

"My Words Create Worlds."

"I Allow My Voice to Be Heard."

VI.   Third Eye Chakra: "I See Through the Consciousness of God"

Location: center of the forehead, between the brows

Color: indigo or violet

Element: light/thought

Associated glands/systems: pineal gland, brain, nervous system, eyes

The Third Eye is the seat of inner vision and expanded perception. It governs intuition, insight, foresight, and imagination. But more than that, it holds the holographic blueprint of your reality—what you believe, you see.

This chakra interfaces with the pineal gland, an ancient crystalline structure known in mysticism as the "seat of the soul." When clear, the third eye allows you to perceive energy, receive divine guidance, and view through the lens of higher truth.

Distortions arise from fear-based programming, illusion, media overload, toxic environments, and trauma that fractured your ability to trust what you know.

Signs of imbalance:

Mental fog or over-intellectualizing

Headaches or pressure in forehead

Nightmares or dream suppression

Fear of the unseen or disconnection from intuition

Reliance on logic over inner guidance

Sacred practices:

Decalcify and activate the pineal gland (sun-gazing, clean water, breathwork)

Practice stillness and observe your thoughts without attachment

Journal your dreams and visions

Meditate with amethyst, labradorite, or fluorite

Ask, "How can I see through my own perceptual illusions?"

Advanced insight:

The Third Eye contains holographic overlays of personal and collective realities. When activated, you begin to project and collapse timelines, accessing parallel versions of yourself and multidimensional consciousness. You are then also able to see how different timelines or states of consciousness overlap and interconnect with all. You also start to attune to the higher subtle frequencies of the higher dimensional planes of existence.

Affirmations:

"I Trust My Inner Vision."

"I See Truth Beyond Appearances."

"My Intuition Is Clear and Reliable."

"I Perceive Through the Eyes of Love."

"I Am a Seer of the Divine."

"I Allow Myself to See Through the Consciousness of God"

VII.   Crown Chakra: "I Know That I Am All That Is"

Location: top of the head

Color: violet, white, or iridescent diamond light

Element: spirit/cosmic intelligence

Associated glands/systems: pineal gland, cerebral cortex, nervous system

The Crown Chakra is your direct connection to God—the Source of all that is, and it is in fact incorruptible. However, it will only open as much as we allow or bound up, the more we allow ourselves to connect to the consciousness of God, the more we allow our Crown Chakra to open, thus activating our divine mind. The Crown Chakra governs your ability to receive divine inspiration, cosmic wisdom, and multidimensional light. When fully open, the Crown becomes a halo of illumination, activating states of bliss, unity, and divine remembrance.

Rather than being "in the sky," the Crown is where Heaven descends through you. It is not about escaping Earth—it is about embodying the infinite while walking in form.

Spiritual bypassing, disillusionment, depression, or fear of surrender can block this chakra. It's also where the ego clings to identity and tries to "earn" enlightenment through effort.

Signs of imbalance:

Disconnection from God/Source

Depression, apathy, or cynicism

Obsession with spiritual perfection or purity

Migraines or crown/head pressure

126

Lack of meaning, purpose, or joy

Sacred practices:

Silent meditation or surrender-based prayer

Connect with white lotus, frankincense, or sandalwood oils

Work with selenite, clear quartz, amethyst, or apophyllite

Visualize golden/white light pouring into your crown

Offer yourself as a vessel of divine will each day

Advanced insight:

The Crown holds the key to white flame consciousness—the awareness that you are the field of God itself. When fully opened, this chakra allows DNA activations, lightbody upgrades, and integration of divine codes from your galactic oversoul, or higher/highest self.

Affirmations:

"I Am One with God."

"Divine Intelligence Flows Through Me Freely."

"I Am A Vessel Of God's Light and Consciousness."

"I Remember Who I Am."

"I Am Infinite."

VIII.   Beyond the Body: The Higher Dimensional Chakras

As we ascend in consciousness and begin to remember our divine origins, higher layers of our energy field begin to activate. These are not just extensions of the seven-chakra system—they are conscious gateways to our soul lineage, star ancestry, mission codes, and universal communion.

While the seven primary chakras govern the human experience, these next chakras anchor you into your eternal self. You begin to remember: you are not just in a body. You are a vast field of light woven into the stars, the Earth, and the Divine Mind.

Earth Star Chakra: "I Am Anchored to the Living Earth"

Location: ~7–12 inches below the feet

Color: deep brown, black, or copper-gold

Element: crystalline earth & magnetic field

Function: ancestral connection, planetary grounding, Earth grid interface

The Earth Star Chakra is not located in the body, but below it—anchoring you to Gaia's crystalline core. This chakra connects you to the soul of the Earth, the Akasha of the land, your ancestral DNA, and the magnetic grid of the planet.

It is through this chakra that you ground your light body, release karmic density, and sync your biofield with Earth's ascension. It carries the codes of your Earth walk—your agreements with the land, the lineages you incarnated through, and your stewardship as a divine being in human form.

When this chakra is activated, you feel a deeper sense of belonging—not just to your body, but to this world. Your energy no longer floats or fragments. It roots with sacred purpose.

Practices for activation:

Grounding barefoot with intentional breath

Honoring your ancestors and lineage with offerings or prayer

Connecting to sacred sites or ley lines

Meditating with black tourmaline, hematite, smoky quartz, or obsidian

Listening to drumming or deep Earth resonant tones

Affirmations:

"I Am Anchored to the Sacred Earth."

"I Honor the Ancestors Who Walked Before Me."

"I Am Grounded, Rooted, and Protected."

"The Earth Supports My Highest Path."

"My Presence Nourishes the Planet."

Soul Star Chakra: "I Am the Light of the Oversoul"

Location: ~6–12 inches above the crown

Color: opalescent white, platinum, iridescent gold

Element: ether/divine intelligence

Function: soul contracts, star lineage, divine remembrance

The Soul Star Chakra is the bridge to your higher self and oversoul. It holds the records of your soul's journey across lifetimes—your gifts, agreements, lessons, and divine purpose.

When activated, it begins to dissolve the illusion of separation, allowing downloads of light, higher intuition, and inner knowing to flow. This is where Akashic remembrance becomes embodied. Where soul fragments reunite. Where you begin to operate as a multidimensional being—guided not by ego, but by divine will.

You may begin to recall dreams, receive guidance in sacred symbols, or feel the presence of soul families and star beings who walk with you.

Practices for activation:

Connecting with your star family or higher self through meditation

Extreme Shadow Work on multidimensional overlays

Working with celestite, selenite, danburite, or herkimer diamond

Practicing light language or energy transmission

Praying to be shown your true soul mission

Laying under the stars and tuning into the frequencies beyond light

Affirmations:

"I Am Guided by the Wisdom of My Soul."

"I Trust the Divine Intelligence Moving Through Me."

"My Higher Self Walks Beside Me in Every Moment."

"I Am the Light Remembering Itself."

"My Purpose Is Divine and Clear."

Galactic Chakra: "I Am a Vessel of Cosmic Light"

Location: ~12–24 inches above the Soul Star

Color: rainbow diamond light/ultraviolet/crystalline gold

Element: pure infinite source intelligence consciousness

Function: galactic lineage, unity consciousness, divine architecture

The Galactic Chakra opens the gate to cosmic unity, star systems, and God-conscious design. This is where the soul begins integrating its galactic mission, divine technologies, and multidimensional structures of light. Here, you move beyond personal soul evolution and begin participating in planetary and cosmic restoration.

When this chakra activates, you begin to remember yourself not just as a soul, but as a light architect, a builder of worlds, a part of the sacred orchestra of the universe.

You may receive star codes, advanced downloads, or visions of your soul working in other realms. This chakra often catalyzes light language, gridwork missions, energy healing upgrades, and divine transmission abilities.

Practices for activation:

Full surrender of all physical, mental, emotional and spiritual projections

Meditation with intention to receive galactic downloads

Lightbody work with diamond codes, platinum rays: rose gold flame, emerald flame, violet flame, blue flame, white flame

Crystals: moldavite, meteorite, tektite, lemurian quartz, celestite

Co-creating with God for planetary healing

Affirmations:

"I Am a Divine Expression of the Infinite Cosmos."

"I Remember My Galactic Origins."

"I Channel Light Across All Dimensions."

"My Body is a Temple of Cosmic Intelligence."

"I Am the Living Bridge Between Heaven and Earth."

"I Am that I Am."

The chakra system is not just a map of your energy—it is a living library of your soul's unfolding. As you awaken each center, you don't just balance energy. You reclaim parts of yourself lost through time, trauma, and forgetfulness.

Whether you are just beginning your healing or have walked lifetimes as a teacher, your chakras will always meet you where you are. With every breath, with every intention, they open—inviting you home again to the truth: you are the light of God. You are the temple of the Divine. You are remembering.

Numerology: The Living Language of Light

There is a language older than words, more ancient than even the stars—a system of intelligence so pure, so precise, it threads through every atom in existence. This is the language of numbers.

Numbers are not merely tools for measurement or math. In their truest form, they are frequencies of consciousness—living, breathing codes within the matrix of reality itself. They shape geometry. They organize time. They unlock memory. And when we learn to read them, we begin to remember who we are, why we came, and how to navigate this holographic experience with intention.

Numerology is the art of decoding these divine patterns. It's how we uncover the architecture behind the veil. But more than that—it's how we co-create with God through the language of light.

I. Birth Dates and Locations: Encoded Portals of Purpose

The day you were born, the place you were born, the precise breath you took to enter this world—none of it is random. Your birth date is a cosmic timestamp. It marks the vibrational frequency of your soul's entry point. It's a key.

Your day of birth often holds your core life lesson or archetype.

Your month reflects the seasonal energy and elemental tone of your incarnation.

Your year reveals the collective vibration you came to serve within and what generational programs or upgrades you're helping to alchemize.

Even the location you were born into is energetically specific. Certain places on Earth are linked to ley lines, ancestral gates, planetary nodal points, or elemental expressions (fire mountains, water cities, air altitudes, earth-heavy regions). You were born where you were not only for personal growth, but to leave energetic imprints and receive activations hidden in the land itself.

Your birth is not an arrival—it is an agreement. Your numbers help you remember the terms.

II.   Repeating Numbers: When Infinite Intelligence Knocks at Your Door

You're going about your day and the clock says 11:11. Your receipt total is 44.44.

The license plate in front of you reads 222-ZEN. You smile. You feel something: a whisper from beyond.

These moments are not coincidences—they are divine checkpoints, echoes from your higher self, nudges from Source reminding you to tune in. Every repeating number you encounter is a frequency pulse, a subtle invitation to awaken a part of you that may be waiting to be experienced.

Below are common sequences and their energetic interpretations—not as rigid definitions, but as guiding signatures:

111 – Initiation; portal opening; your thoughts are shaping reality—immediately

222 – Partnership, polarity, divine duality; peace is being woven beneath the surface

333 – Trinity codes; support from the higher realms; creativity and communication awakening

444 – Angelic stabilization; you are building something real; stay grounded

555 – Chaos before rebirth; change is sacred; let go

666 – Realignment; come home to the truth; balance matter and spirit

777 – Soul mastery; inner wisdom remembered; clair-senses awakening

888 – Infinity loop; prosperity; karmic return; step into your harvest

999 – Completion; graduation. end of a karmic contract. time to release

000 – The divine void; the reset; a return to Source; the infinite present moment

Beyond these, you may begin to receive more nuanced combinations, personalized to your soul:

171 – The path of God's will anchored into your human steps

979 – End of a soul chapter; gateway to a higher octave of service

626 – Inner union codes; heart-led stability after emotional storm

848 – Infinite wisdom harmonizing with empowered stability

313 – A divine balance between expression and reflection, giving and receiving

Each number is a mirror—reflecting where you are, what you're integrating, and what's being offered if you choose to step or drive through it.

Divine Download: MPH Signs as Stargates: Driving Through Activations

There was a moment, during a drive one afternoon when I realized I wasn't just on the highway, I was passing through a series of vibrational gateways! We are always in a state of creation whether or not we are conscious of it. So, I was asked to play with the signs on the parkway.

The miles per hour signs, usually ignored or obeyed unconsciously, suddenly lit up like signals. Each one vibrated with a specific frequency. With it came a message, a chance to set an intention, pull in a new timeline, or anchor light codes into the Earth.

When we're driving on the parkway, there are usually MPH signs on both sides of you as you pass. It was at this moment that I realized we can utilize the mundane and make it magical. These signs act as markers for grounding activation sequences, and being that they are on either side of you while you drive, you are quite literally driving through a portal of energy. Part of this life experience is about play, it's about learning how we are able to manipulate energy. So, I decided to give it a try, what's the worst that could happen right? Turns out two weeks later, I ended up manifesting one of the greatest events and highest paying events I had done since starting to offer Reiki & Readings!

I. Signs and Symbolism: Co-Creation with Physical Form

35 MPH – (3+5 = 8) Strength, inner stability, and karmic integration; a moment to pause and root into what you're building, divine driven change

40 MPH – Foundation and structure (4) with all possibilities (0); foundational reset

45 MPH – (4+5=9) Completion; completing cycles with stability (4) and transformation/change (5)

50 MPH – Transformation (5) with all possible potentials (0)

55 MPH – Divine change; acceleration toward higher timelines; let the old shed

65 MPH – (6+5 = 11) Master number, higher dimensional gateways, anchoring higher levels of consciousness all with balance (6) and transformation (5); gateway energy; use this to send light, make declarations, or consciously shift your reality

Every time you see one of these signs, breathe, set the intention that as you pass through these numerological portals you are anchoring in the highest good of all. The most important thing is to FEEL how it would feel when you have already attained what it is you were hoping to manifest as if you are currently experiencing it.. Say something out loud or within that matches the energy you wish to bring forward. Here are some examples:

At 40 MPH: "I reset my foundation. I am safe to begin again."

At 50 MPH: "I choose the highest path forward with grace and presence."

At 55 MPH: "I allow the old to fall away. I trust this acceleration."

At 65 MPH: "I open the portal of 11. I walk through in divine timing."

In this way, the road becomes a ceremonial runway. You are not just driving—you are consciously navigating through frequencies, leaving energetic footprints with every mile.

You become the priestess, the architect, the divine architect on wheels.

Reality: A Playground for Divine Communication

What if the entire matrix of your life was a sacred interactive oracle? What if the stoplight, the apartment number, the time you wake up, and the distance you walk were all part of a cosmic choreography designed to respond to your consciousness?

Numbers, signs, symbols, animals, and people show up to reflect and to help us co-create. When you become aware of them, you begin to shift timelines, unlock encoded gifts, and activate healing, not just for yourself, but for everyone connected to your field.

This is why I began using repeating highway signs or number combos as intentional grid anchors while driving. I like to set abundance intentions every time I see dollar signs while walking through a store, not just for myself, but for the entire collective. I create mini portals at mile markers 44.4, sending protection to all travelers.

When you tap and tune into the consciousness around you, you begin to move through life as a conscious architect of reality—using the language of this universe to guide, align, and elevate everything around you.

You don't have to be a numerologist to create with numbers or the reality around you. You already are part of it. Numbers, just like people, animals and even places are a living transmission, speaking through frequency. They are tools for us and we can use them to:

Set intentions for energy at specific times (9:09, 2:22, 5:55)

Create symbolic activation codes for rituals or prayers

Decode birthdates, years, and locations for soul contracts

Build sacred geometries (triads, spirals, master number clusters)

Open personal portals and activate healing grids

You are not separate from the intelligence behind all that is, it is a part of you! You are the code. You are the key. You are the bridge. You are a co-creator.

So, the next time you see 11:11 or drive past a 65 MPH sign, don't just see it as a sign, see it as a chance to create. Remember, you are allowed and supposed to have fun!

Sacred Sound: Tuning the Soul Through Frequency

If numbers are the code behind creation, then sound is the breath of those codes made manifest.

Sound is more than vibration—it is a living current of intelligence that can shift realities, restore harmony, and awaken the sleeping parts of the soul. In the beginning, "the Word," God's sonic waves, moved across the void and gave birth to form. Light became sound. Sound became matter. Matter took form..

To work with sound is to work with the original blueprint of God.

Every cell, every organ, every emotion and thought in the human body responds to sound. This is not poetic—it is biological and spiritual truth. Our bodies are symphonic instruments, composed of crystalline structures and electromagnetic circuits designed to receive and transmit frequencies. When we are in harmony, we vibrate with health, clarity, and divine rhythm. When we fall out of tune, incoherence can manifest as pain, confusion, or illness—mentally, emotionally, physically, or spiritually.

Sound can restore harmony. Not metaphorically—literally.

The Anatomy of Sound and the Human Body System

Your body is not solid. It is a fluid system of oscillating particles—an instrument, fine-tuned by nature and divinely coded to respond to vibration. Every organ resonates at its own frequency. Your heart has a tone. Your bones, your glands, your brainwaves, and your nervous system each sing their own song.

Your thoughts emit frequency. Your emotions create resonance fields. Your voice projects your current state of truth into the space around you. The sounds you speak—or suppress—reverberate through the tissues of your body, shaping your reality.

Low-frequency sounds (fear, guilt, shame) constrict energy and create distortion.

High-frequency sounds (love, gratitude, joy) expand energy and open the channels of divine flow.

This is why sound healing works. It bypasses the intellect and speaks directly to the soul through sensation. No belief is required. When the right frequency is received, the body remembers how to heal. It reorganizes itself around divine harmony.

Solfeggio Frequencies: Sacred Tones of Creation

Among the most powerful and ancient tones are the Solfeggio frequencies—a set of mathematically precise sound frequencies that were said to be used in Gregorian chants and early sacred music. Each tone carries a specific healing quality and connects to different aspects of the physical and spiritual body.

Here are the core Solfeggio tones:

174 Hz – Pain relief and physical healing; grounding and cellular regeneration

285 Hz – Repairing tissues and organs; energizing the blueprint of the body

396 Hz – Liberating guilt and fear; transmuting root chakra imbalances

417 Hz – Undoing situations and facilitating change; healing trauma stored in the sacral

528 Hz – DNA repair and miracles; activates solar plexus, love, and transformation

639 Hz – Harmonizing relationships; reconnecting heart-centered unity

741 Hz – Awakening intuition; cleansing infection; detoxing negativity

852 Hz – Returning to spiritual order; activating third eye and divine guidance

963 Hz – Pineal gland activation; merging with the God frequency; crown chakra gateway

You can listen to these tones in meditation, during sleep, in body treatments, or simply as background resonance in your space. You don't have to understand how they work. Your soul already does. They remind your system of the harmony that was present before distortion ever began.

I.   How Sound Heals: The Four Levels

1. Physically

Sound penetrates tissue. It vibrates water molecules. It stimulates circulation, reduces inflammation, and can reset the nervous system. Even ultrasound—a common medical tool—is a form of sound frequency used to stimulate healing and view the unseen. Singing bowls, tuning forks, drumming, and humming all create vibrations that affect fascia, lymph, and even cellular memory.

2. Emotionally

Emotions are frequency based. A single tone can access buried emotions without needing to relive trauma. Vocalizing (chanting, moaning, or singing freely) can release stored tension. Sound helps process grief, soften fear, and restore peace where words fail.

3. Mentally

Certain frequencies (like 528 Hz or binaural beats) can shift brainwave states—taking you out of anxiety-ridden beta states and into alpha, theta, or delta waves associated with meditation, intuition, and regeneration.

4. Spiritually

Sound is one of the fastest ways to shift into higher consciousness. Chanting names of God, speaking sacred mantras, singing from the soul—these are not religious acts; they are vibrational alignments that open the inner temple, allow one to access higher states of consciousness, and create coherence in the mind body spirit connection.

II. Toning and Vocal Healing: Becoming the Instrument

Your voice is your most personal sound tool. It carries the resonance of your truth, your power, and your prayer. Toning is the practice of allowing single sustained vowel sounds to move through the body. You can target any chakra or organ system with a simple intention and a tone.

Ahhh for the heart

Ommm for crown and grounding

Eeeee for third eye and clarity

Ohhh for root and anchoring

Uuuu for deep womb and sacral activation

Even simple humming can stimulate the vagus nerve, calm the nervous system, and regulate emotions.

When we tone, chant, or sing—not for performance, but for presence—we create a bridge between our inner and outer world. We become both the instrument and the music and, in that moment, we ascend.

III. Anchoring Healing Through Sound: Practical Integration

You can begin using sound in your daily spiritual or healing practice with profound results:

During bodywork, meditations or Reiki sessions: play healing frequencies or gently hum over energy centers

In emotional release: tone into the area of pain, and allow the sound to express the stuck emotion: allow yourself to moan or scream with the release

Before meditation: chant a single word or phrase (e.g., "I Am") and let the vibration open the space

While cleansing space: use bells, bowls, clapping, or light language to reset the energy field

While setting intentions: speak them aloud, slowly and with reverence, allowing the words to carry vibration into form

Remember: sound is not bound by time. You can send it across timelines. You can embed it into objects, plants, crystals, and even into your own voice notes or recordings for later healing.

You are the tuning fork. You are the vessel. You are the voice of God in motion.

Light Language: The Soul's Native Sound

There may come a point on your journey when you begin speaking or toning sounds that are not from your known vocabulary. This is not madness—it is memory. It is light language.

Light language is a multidimensional, frequency-based expression of your soul. It bypasses the linear mind and speaks directly to the divine intelligence within others and within the field. It may come as sounds, tones, clicks, chirps, chants, or ancient syllables. Sometimes it is sung. Sometimes it is spoken in waves. It activates light codes in your DNA and in others.

You may not know what it means, but you will feel what it does. Light language is not about translation. It is about transmission.

Some use it to activate healing. Others use it to unlock soul memory. Many channel it through sacred tones, through movement, or while doing bodywork. If this begins to open within you, allow it. Trust it. It is God speaking through your voice.

I.   Sound and the Gateway to Higher Consciousness

The universe is not silent. Galaxies spiral with harmony. Atoms hum. Trees chant in root songs. Planets emit tones so vast we cannot hear them with our ears, but our souls remember their songs.

When you work with sound, you are not simply healing—you are re-attuning yourself to the divine symphony. Sound aligns you with cosmic rhythms. It restores balance not just in the body, but in the blueprint of who you truly are.

When used intentionally, sound becomes a key, a code, a bridge. It awakens. It dissolves illusion. It opens the portals to higher levels of consciousness and carries you across them.

So sing. Tone. Speak your truth. Let your voice vibrate with freedom and divine intelligence. Because in every sacred sound, a piece of God returns home—through you.

Sound opens the doorway—but dreams invite us in. Once our frequency is attuned through tone, vibration, and resonance, the soul begins to speak in a different language: symbols, sensations, visions, and story. What was once felt through the body as sound now becomes seen through the soul as a dream. It's all connected—just a shift in form. One vibrates through the nervous system, the other travels through the astral body. After the sound fades, the dreaming begins. And in that sacred silence, we cross the threshold into a realm just as real, just as holy—the space where Spirit teaches us while we sleep.

Dreams & the Astral Realms: Healing While You Sleep

As we attune to the subtle frequencies of sound, our inner world begins to open wider until we find ourselves on the edge of another sacred realm, the astral.

Dreams are not illusions. They are not meaningless flickers of the subconscious. Dreams are portals. They are living, breathing messages from the soul, a nightly meeting place between spirit and soul, a multidimensional bridge connecting past, present, and future selves.

Every time we close our eyes to rest, we cross into an astral space that holds memory, symbolism, divine dialogue, past lives, future timelines, and soul contracts all layered into one. In this space, linear time collapses. We process unspoken emotions. We receive prophecy and we encounter both our shadows and guides. We dream to remember.

I.   Why We Dream

Dreaming is the soul's way of digesting reality—both what has happened and what is yet to come.

Some dreams show us our subconscious patterns—thoughts and emotions still unresolved. Some reflect deep soul work—past life fragments resurfacing to be healed. Some are downloads—insights or messages from your guides or higher self. Others are shared classrooms with our soul family, where we co-learn in non-physical space.

Every dream is multilayered. A dream can carry emotional healing, symbolic coding, spiritual teaching, and literal precognition all at once. That's why interpreting dreams isn't about decoding symbols like a dictionary—it's about feeling into the message your soul is trying to show you.

II.   Astral Realms and the Astral Body: The Vehicle of the Soul Between Worlds

To understand the dream realm more deeply, we must understand where it exists: the astral plane.

The astral realm is a dimension that exists between the physical and the purely spiritual. It is a world of energy and form, where thoughts take shape, emotions have texture, and soul experiences unfold beyond the limitations of linear time or gravity.

This is the dimension you enter each night when your body sleeps and your astral body—your luminous, etheric counterpart—travels.

Your astral body is your consciousness in motion. It's subtle, light-based, and vibrationally attuned to explore other planes. It can:

Attend meetings with soul family and guides

Heal emotional wounds through symbolic experiences

Revisit past lives or parallel incarnations

Access higher teachings

Experience prophecy

Visit other planetary realms, timelines, or dimensions

Some call it lucid dreaming, others call it astral projection. In truth, we all travel in the astral—consciously or unconsciously..

The vividness of your dream often correlates with how consciously you're navigating the astral. The more grounded and open you are, the more clearly you remember your astral experiences.

The astral realms are not just "dream worlds." They are training grounds, healing temples, initiation chambers, and reunion halls for the soul. Some places are fluid, formed by collective thought. Others are fixed, high vibrational zones that exist across lifetimes.

Some—especially in turbulent dreams—reflect the lower astral: spaces of emotional residue, collective fear, and ancestral trauma. These dreams often invite clearing, courage, and protection practices.

III.   How to Strengthen Your Connection to the Astral Body

Daily meditation calms the physical mind and strengthens the subtle field

Sleep hygiene (no electronics before bed, grounding practices, sacred space) sharpens dream clarity

Set an intention before sleep: "I call in clarity, healing, and conscious recall"

Take intention setting baths for dream recall prior to sleep with salt and baking soda added to the tub, crystals are a great addition as well, be sure the crystal is water safe.

Use crystals like labradorite, Iolite, super seven, moonstone, selenite, and amethyst under your pillow

Journal upon waking—even a single word holds a thread

Ask your guides to walk beside you during astral journeys

Speak your dreams aloud—vibration re-anchors the wisdom into your body

As we continue to evolve spiritually, our dreams become more than reflections. They become realms of spiritual responsibility—places where we can send healing, dissolve karma, receive assignments, and help others even while we sleep.

The Firmament of Consciousness: Navigating the Waters Above and Below

In the sacred texts, it is written that God created the firmament to divide the waters above from the waters below. For many, this has been interpreted through a literal lens—a structural sky, a barrier, a boundary between heaven and Earth. But, as I sat with this scripture in meditation, I was shown something deeper. The firmament is not just physical. It is energetic. It is the consciousness of the mind.

The "waters above" are the higher emotions—love, compassion, unity, peace, divine bliss. The "waters below" are the lower emotions—fear, grief, anger, judgment, shame. And the firmament? The firmament is our awareness. It is the lens through which we process and perceive both.

Just like Earth is surrounded by the atmosphere, we too are surrounded by thought forms, beliefs, memories, and programs. These energetic layers create a type of dome around our perception. And through this dome—the firmament—we must navigate the emotional waters in order to return to God.

The waters above nourish the soul. They are where higher consciousness flows freely and where sacred intelligence becomes available to us. The waters below, however, must be purified. These are the stagnant emotions, the traumas, the denser frequencies that cloud our clarity. They aren't evil, they are part of the journey. But if we live solely beneath the firmament, trapped in the lower waters of fear and illusion, we remain cut off from divine remembrance.

To ascend is not to escape the lower waters, it is to consciously move through them. To feel. To heal. To integrate. As we do, our consciousness expands. The firmament thins. We no longer perceive separation between the emotional realm and the divine realm. We begin to see that they were never truly separate at all.

The waters above and below are not two different things. They are one spectrum. And the firmament is the veil we must learn to part. This is the same veil spoken of in the Holy of Holies, the same veil torn when Christ released his spirit. It is symbolic of the final separation between man and God being dissolved.

We are the firmament. We are the gatekeepers of perception and our task is to become conscious of which waters we are swimming in. Are we reacting from the depths of the lower waters, or are we flowing from the wisdom of the higher?

When the firmament of the mind becomes clear—through prayer, meditation, emotional alchemy, and spiritual truth—we become conduits for both realms. We unify the waters. We walk as living bridges. Heaven and Earth converge within us.

Recognize that your emotional experiences are not random or wrong. They are like water. And like water, they are meant to move, to be purified, to be honored. When you do this, you rise above the storm. You become the stillness between the waves.

And in that stillness, you remember:

Your mind is the firmament.

And the waters—above and below—are yours to master.

Spirit's Spotlight: Encoded Dreams & Downloads, A Divine Dialogue

In the following section I have included downloads, dreams, and transmissions that I have been guided to share with the collective. These act as encoded teachings. It has been titled Spirit's Spotlight, serving as a reminder that these dreams, downloads, and transmissions were not meant only for me, but instead they came to illuminate something for all of us. These are multidimensional activations.

Dreams are not just for our entertainment, they are also to help our consciousness evolve. They hold coded lessons, emotional healing, spiritual assignment, and soul memory codes which serve as activations for you. Some dreams are very specific, while others much more symbolic.

When you begin to honor your dreams, you become more than a dreamer. You become a co-creator, not just for your world, but for others as well. You become a conscious navigator of the invisible, making what was hidden come to light. A bridge between dimensions, connecting and guiding others as well as yourself back home to God, back home to all that is.

I. "School and The Glasses" – Perception, Oneness, and Earth
School

This dream, which was described earlier, took place in a symbolic classroom, just as our experience on earth is a place of learning. Through the shifting of my glasses, I was shown how our perception creates reality. What we believe is what we project; what we believe is what we experience. This dream reminded me that the lenses we wear are shaped by our level of consciousness which is the baseline for our beliefs, and what we choose to perceive becomes our reality or truth. When the glasses came off in the dream, there was no separation, I was still in the omnipresent infinite essence of God, our home.

The collective message: you are still home, you are always with God; you were never separate, you just believed yourself to be. When you change the lenses of which you are perceiving your world through, then your world will change.

II. "The Doorway of Forgiveness" – A Transmission

"What if the reason people aren't healing… isn't because of them? What if it's because of you?"

When I first heard this come through, I was curious, not judgmental towards myself, so I wondered how I could view this from a higher perspective.

If people are mirroring my beliefs, and I believe that they are not capable of healing, then I in turn create an energetic boundary or barrier for them to have to work through. When multiple people think or feel the same way about someone or something, it creates a layered web of energy around them or it, each layer consisting of another's projection. These projections can then be amplified by the internal beliefs of the person who is being judged, thereby quantifying the amount of energy projected by that field of energy or consciousness of said judgment surrounding the person or thing. If we allow ourselves to take responsibility for our projections or judgements upon others, then we allow for the energy or projection of that consciousness to be cleared from within ourselves as well as the other person. This in turn gives the person or thing being judged an open doorway to walk through for transformation. Forgiveness is a doorway, a portal, not just for self-liberation, but for clearing your field and the field around others.

The collective message: every interaction is an opportunity to create, you can choose to create a wall or a door. It is always your choice. Forgiveness allows for doors to be built where there were once walls. Forgiveness isn't just love—it is an act of God, mastery, an act of service, and sacred liberation. Forgiveness allows transmutation, forgiveness allows change, forgiveness is a portal to higher levels of consciousness.

III.   "As We Change, So Do the Earth's Landscapes"

This dream came to me at a time when I was asking for clarity about the world—about ascension, family, about navigating this life through chaotic times.

This dream opened with me getting off of a plane on a tropical island. I could tell it was a tropical area based on the temperature of the dream, the lush vegetation, the crystal clear, aqua-blue water off in the distance. I had just landed in paradise, or so I thought. My entire family was with me in this dream. I gathered in the lobby of the resort with my family, and then a sense of urgency fell over me. I was aware that an active chain of volcanoes loomed nearby on the lower east side of the island preparing to erupt.

The volcano symbolically represented repressed emotional energy—both personal and collective—building beneath the surface. The kind of energy we think we've buried or ignored long enough to disappear, but it's still simmering. This volcano was the symbolic eruption of everything we've tried to suppress: fear, unspoken truth, grief, rage, et cetera.

I felt the land begin to tilt underneath my feet, the ground started to tremble, and I knew we had to get out of there. The illusion of balance was gone, and we were no longer on stable ground. I now

170

understand this to be the moment when we realized the world we've built—our systems, our beliefs, our habits, our thought processes, our routines—was never built on stable ground. It was built from a place of fear or as a traumatic response, instead of intuitively guided by God or our higher selves. It was never built upon stable ground, but most don't notice until their foundations begin to crumble.

There was a lake nearby. I had a memory of it being extremely beautiful, crystal clear, and able to be traversed. As we approached it, I noticed the waters were murky, and the entire lake had become invaded with crocodiles. As I was standing near the edge, a crocodile swiped me with its tail and I plunged into the lake. Thrashing to get myself to the surface, I am met face to face with the crocodile. Its presence was a clear symbol: an invasion of the sacred. The lake, which once represented calm emotional waters and spiritual peace, had become dangerous. Crocodiles are ancient, primal survival energies— shadow forces. They represent latent fears, subconscious survival instincts, and spiritual attacks that come when we aren't grounded in truth. I grabbed its head and wrapped myself around its body attempting to hold it down under the water while I tried to wedge a stick in its mouth. My intention was not to hurt or kill it, I just wanted to try to get it to stop attacking me. It didn't work; it just kept coming at me. I grabbed the right side of its head and drove the stick under its chin, through its mouth and I watched as it pierced through the head. I had to silence the energy of fear by using discernment and divine force. This moment taught me that peace doesn't mean passivity. Sometimes peace means knowing when to stand in sacred protection.

I quickly jumped back onto the platform and ran back to my family. I found them in the resort and told them that we were going to have to leave all of our belongings behind. There wouldn't be enough time to grab anything or enough room on the plane for anything except for the clothes on our backs. I knew there were planes that were preparing to take us all to safety, but these planes were taking off from container ships that were 10,000 feet in the air. This didn't strike me as odd when I was explaining it to them, I just knew we had to get up there somehow.

As I shifted my focus to finding an exit from the resort, I realized that we were in fact very high up in the building. First, we had to find a way safely down. I saw a girl waiting for the elevators to come, but I told her it was of no avail. The elevator carts were going out of control, crashing down from the top and then shooting back up again. Sometimes the doors would open to just the elevator shaft, nothing to actually step into. I reminded her it wasn't a good idea to try and fast track it down, it would be better to take the steps. This was clearly about the artificial "ascension" systems we think will carry us—money, institutions, social media platforms, false leadership. Some no longer work or worse, they open to nowhere. Discernment is the exit strategy.

We ran to the stairwell, opened the door and looked in amazement at the layout of the stairs. They descended downward in a spiral, they were floating stairs made of obsidian, which only became visible after

172

you took a step forward. They were steep and unsafe by design, and that in itself was the message: the true path of ascension isn't glamorous. It's uncertain and it requires your full presence and your full surrender. The girl I was with was moving so ridiculously slow, I pleaded with her to move faster, but she just grinned at me as she lugged a giant suitcase down the stairs with her. Without hesitation, I grabbed the suitcase with my right hand and grabbed her arm with my left hand. I continued downward while I carried this girl's suitcase and guided her along as gently as I could. That part of the dream reminded me that awakening is rarely done alone. We help carry each other home while carrying ourselves. I turned my head to face forward and the stairs turned into a corridor. I turned the corner and saw someone had left their car keys. There was a light and a shadow-being reaching for the keys. I realized this was a representation of our choice to allow ourselves to be led by light or shadow. I grabbed the keys and handed them to the light-being.

Instantly, I was transported outside to a glass balcony area which overlooks the ocean. Behind me was an infinity pool and to the left was my older sister, Jessica. As I looked out to the ocean, I saw a tsunami wave approaching us. I gasped as I grabbed my sister's arm. She asked what was wrong as I pointed out to the ocean. I told her this tsunami was heading right towards us and if we didn't move, we were going to be swept away. She reminded me that there's no way the tsunami was coming because the earth we were standing on had already tilted 45 degrees, it was actually flowing parallel to us. It only looked like a threat because of my perspective. This is one of the most powerful truths: your perspective shapes your reality.

I showed my sister the keys and told her we needed to grab the rest of the family and drive to the bus point. There were buses waiting for us and others to arrive to take us to the container ships and planes. We grabbed our family from the infinity pool and ran to the front doors, but when we opened the doors, it led to a bathroom. I saw other people there completely unaware of the impending doom, and when I tried to alert them, they seemed to be completely unphased. Some were even playing in the toilet water, I couldn't understand why they did not want to get out of the path of destruction.

I turned to my right and found another door which led outside. I ran as fast as I could thinking my family would follow right behind me. When I turned around, I saw they weren't there. They didn't follow me like I thought they would, so turned around and ran back into the resort building to gather them.

I managed to gather them all and lead them through another door I had found, and, as we were walking out of the resort, my mom said that there was a cab coming for us and we should probably just wait for it. I told her I had a car waiting for us already and we just needed to get to it; we didn't have time to wait for someone else to get a cab to us. We had a ride already and we needed to go NOW!

I noticed while walking that I was chewing gum, but the more I chewed, the tougher it became. I managed to blow a few bubbles with this gum, not without it getting all over my face and hair of course, but it all came out easily. One of the bubbles I blew popped all over my entire face, I laughed about it being a face mask to everyone I was with as I peeled it off. The gum represented the pressure of expression, the tension in my voice, the discomfort of holding onto truth when the world feels unstable. Even my laughter became a spiritual act—a way to transmute fear, lighten the load, and move forward.

As we were all walking towards the car to get to the plane, the girl that I found at the elevators took out a video camera and started to film. I had an eerie sense that this would be the last time the land would ever look like this, I knew it was all going to change. As we continued to walk, we came to a field on my left, in the field sat hundreds of people. People sat there calmly. They weren't coming.

I understood they had chosen to stay, not out of ignorance, but out of a soul agreement. They were anchors of peace for those who believed they wouldn't make it. No one was trying to convince them. They were witnessing, holding space, honoring their path, and so I honored them too. I said a silent prayer as I continued towards the car.

I then started to wonder, if your world flips… where do you go? What is considered the safest location? You can't stand on the shore,

175

you'll slide. You can't hide underground, you'll be buried. You can't go in the ocean, you'll drown in a tsunami. Then I woke up…

This dream was an ascension map. A blueprint for what happens when the illusion collapses and the old exits no longer work. Land represents the physical foundations, while water represents the emotional foundations of which we build upon in life. It teaches us that sometimes the fastest way can lead to dead ends or voids. It shows how our perspective shapes the reality which we experience, and is a factor as to how we react to what we are experiencing. It also teaches us that even when the earth shakes and the water rises, your soul will always know how to get to safety, as long as you are willing to trust it.

IV.   "Sky Codes, Star Dragons, and Spiders"

This dream felt more like a galactic transmission

I was outside with my dad and a few others, looking up at the sky. It was dark, but there was a faint hue of violet light peeking through the gray clouds—something about it felt cosmic, as if I were staring into space itself. Then, right in front of us, an object began flying in a

176

perfect infinity pattern, weaving left and right. It wasn't chaotic—it was intentional, precise. As I watched it move, I could feel it activating something in my own field.

I turned back and saw a yellow eye high above me, soft, glowing, almost angelic in its energy, with rays emanating outward. I understood this to be the eye of divine awareness, the presence of God observing, witnessing, and teaching. It showed me that what was happening in the sky wasn't random, it was meant to be observed.

When I turned back to the sky in front of me, the object pierced through the clouds. What had been hidden suddenly revealed itself: a dragon-head shaped spacecraft. It was large and scaly, and its color was a deep royal blue covered in white stars. As it flew, its face shifted with its direction, almost like it was scanning for something while flying in an infinity loop.

But then something changed.

The dragon ship's nose dipped downward, and it began a direct descent toward the Earth. In order for it to change direction, the mouth had to unhinge and slide down. As it descended downward, the ship looked more like a snake's head. When it wanted to change direction and travel up again, its face shifted back up into that of a dragon. And I remember thinking: that's unusual, the head was able to

177

morph completely and now it's coming closer to us. "Interesting," I thought to myself. It's as if the dragon had transformed into a snake as it descended from the upper realms.

Almost immediately, my attention was drawn to the ground. I looked down and to the left and saw a spider glowing with a soft, pale-blue light. It was weaving a web with intricate intelligence as if it had been preparing for this moment for a long time. Suddenly, the spider quickly moved toward me, it jumped toward my face, startled me, and I woke up.

I knew this wasn't just a jump scare dream, there was something deeper, as long as I was willing to work past the fear of the jump scare. As I sat with the dream, the symbolism began to unfold.

The infinity pattern in the sky represented timelessness, the looping nature of lifetimes, reincarnations, and divine multidimensional awareness. It showed me that time is not linear, it's encoded, and when we attune to those patterns, we are able to see the interconnected nature of all that is.

The eye of light was God, or God's consciousness watching, witnessing, and reminding me that I was not just dreaming, I was receiving. It was a moment of divine observation. It was as if I was witnessing an event horizon.

The dragon ship symbolized an ancient, galactic form of wisdom—a merging of the mythical and metaphysical. The symbol of the snake head on its descent, a symbolic reference to a kundalini awakening. While the dragon head upon its ascent, the symbolic reference to the alchemical transmutation of fear into wisdom. Its royal blue color connected it to higher communication and truth, while the stars embedded in it spoke to our divine source origin. Dragons have long been seen as guardians of truth, energy, and codes. In this case, I felt it was bringing light codes—not just to me, but to the planet.

Its descent was important. It wasn't attacking. It wasn't circling. It was coming down intentionally, as if it were delivering something to be received at ground level—an invitation to embody, not escape. Not something to be feared, but something to be in awe of.

The spider was perhaps the most powerful teacher of all. She was showing me the divine web of life, of consciousness—how everything is interwoven beautifully together to support the entire system. Her pale-blue light mirrored the color combination of royal blue and white with a neon glow. She was the representation of the divine feminine, the weaver of destiny, the archetype of creation itself.

And yes, she startled me awake—but in doing so, she activated me. As a child, I was startled to awakening, as scary as those experiences were, they were also the most liberating.

This dream also felt like an initiation into a higher level of perception—one that reminded me that we are all being asked to observe what we are experiencing from higher levels of awareness, not fear. You have the ability to observe everything from a higher perspective or higher consciousness if you allow yourself to do so. This dream also touched on Earth not being isolated, and, in fact, being a part of a multidimensional galactic ecosystem. I would like to note that this dream took place in the beginning of November 2024, later on in that month there would be reports of strange drones flying all over the tri-state area.

V.   "The Tree in the Toilet" — Cleansing Ancestral Karma Through the Root of Emotion

This dream was one of the most viscerally symbolic ancestral clearings I've ever experienced.

I found myself cleaning my mother's bathroom—a mundane task that quickly transformed into something deeply spiritual. The bathroom, a space symbolically tied to release, purification, and private emotions. This alone signaled that this dream was about elimination, ancestral work, and the process of clearing what no longer belongs to us.

The toilet was clogged, she needed help. She tried everything she could, but still was unable to get it cleared. "Don't worry mom, I've got it. I'm the strongest, just watch!" I said to her as I raised a plunger high above my head.

I counted with each push, ONE, TWO, and on THREE out comes huge chunks of dirt flying everywhere, and then a giant tree emerges right from the center of the toilet. There wasn't any foliage on the branches, it reminded me of a tree in the middle of winter–cold, bare, withering. I turned to my mother in amazement and tried to get her attention, but all she was focused on was the mess.

A massive clump of dirt from the toilet bowl was embedded with red stones—red symbolizing root chakra energy, ancestral bloodlines, trauma, and generational wounding. Buried within this clump of dirt was a light and dark blue wallet. Representing the financial ties to the wounding, as well as the necessary color energy needed to assist with transmuting it. The color blue hints at truth and communication—the "wallet" representing hidden or suppressed ancestral wealth, both literal and energetic, now being unearthed.

Attached to the wallet was a small MP3 device, playing the song "Heaven"—a potent symbol. Reminding me that Heaven is always all around me, waiting to be heard, assisting with the healing.

As I started to scrub the metaphysical waste off of the toilet, I knew it wasn't mine. Even the colors shifted—from dirt and brown to white and blue, the toilet literally glowing as the energy transmuted. Blue for communication and healing and white for divine purification. The old residue was gone, and what remained was transformed.

The knowledge of "I didn't create this mess" still echoed loudly in the dream and reflected a truth for many of us: we are clearing generational pain, dysfunction, and energetic imprints that we may have not initiated, but have agreed to release.

An entire tree emerging from a portal of waste. This reminded me of the profound potential for growth. A symbol of what was left to be transmuted. The tree represented ancestral memory, family lines, and DNA. It rose from the same place we typically associate with what we discard. God was showing me we must clear what we carry, we choose everything we carry, we carry it to transmute it for ourselves and for others.

When I shared this revelation with my family in the dream, there was initial resistance. Not resistance in acknowledgement, more so resistance of outside perspectives on how it would look, fear of exposure. Eventually, they all agreed to allow me to share it.

Upon waking from that dream, I could still remember it in very vivid detail, so I made sure I wrote everything down into my phone. Once complete, I was pondering the symbolism of the dream, my focus was on the healing components of the colors. While I was scrubbing the waste in the dream, it was turning from white to shades of blue to white again. The wallet was also a white, light blue, and dark blue color.

I closed my eyes, visualized my mom in my mind, and started seeing her surrounded by white, light blue, and dark blue light. I set the intention that this healing be sent to her entire being as well as ancestral line for the highest good of all. I sent her so much love, and thanked God and my guides for this information. I woke up and went about my day, not thinking anything more of it.

My little sister had texted the group chat a short while later about my mom's outfit selection for the day. Both of my sisters were in Hungary with my mom and dad. I was prepared to join them in a few days. We were all meeting in Hungary for my little sister's graduation from medical school.

My mom's outfit selection included the colors I had dreamt of and sent to her earlier that morning. Her top consisted of white and dark blue stripes, and her red shorts were adorned with light blue and white flowers! She was wearing every color I had sent to her!

I responded to my little sister's message, "Wanna know something wild about her outfit?"

"What," my little sister replied.

I continued, "Last night in my dream, I was shown that mom specifically needs white and blue light to help her heal, and this AM when I woke up, I sent her white and blue light. She is literally dressed in a white and blue top and her shorts also have white and blue flowers!"

My little sister responded, "Jen, I love you but what crack did you smoke?" To which I responded, "Oh Nasike, if you only understood the significance of dreams and what I do with energy work."

I chose to include this dream and my encounter with my family for multiple reasons. First, the significance of the carry over of information, meaning the information that was received during the dream carried over into "real life." The symbolism of the colors, the tree, and the initial resistance was clearly well defined within the dream and also carried over into real life. The physical, mental, or emotional reactions that may be encountered from individuals when relaying information received from a dreamtime or conscious transmission may either match the reactions received within the dreamtime state or be offered as guidelines as to how to move forward.

You may not have made the mess, but you carry the gift to clear it. You may plunge through generations of trauma, but what you will find is a tree of wisdom. What you thought was waste becomes the root of your awakening.

VI.   "You Can See the Future by Being in the Present" — A
       Transmission During Meditation

"You can see the future by being in the present." I heard one
afternoon while in meditation. It was followed by a vision—an
intricate spider's web connecting not just people and events, but
lifetimes, timelines, dimensions, and emotions. The web glistened with
light, expanding upon itself in fractal patterns.

This transmission showed me what happens when we truly
anchor ourselves in the present moment. When we are truly and fully
present, we are able to perceive all thoughts, emotions, and energies
within and around us, thus allowing one to accurately predict or
understand the nature of events that are to unfold. Therefore being
able to see or predict the future. When we allow ourselves to fully
engage with the present moment, true activation of higher timelines
and consciousness happens. For you choose to observe that which is
of higher timelines, higher consciousness, or of higher good; therefore,
you choose to create it. It is not something we reach for—it is
something we anchor.

The more we allow ourselves to activate God's consciousness into
our consciousness within each moment, the more we allow ourselves
and others the chance to change into higher versions of themselves or
ascend to higher levels of consciousness. Each wound, each event,

each relationship, each conversation, each act, whether known or unknown, is waiting for you to pour God's consciousness into it.

This is the sacred undercurrent of the Age of Aquarius: The Water Bearer.

The sacred water bearing, pouring the living waters of God's consciousness into every moment.

Your Return Home

You've journeyed through the energy centers of your body. You've learned to decode numbers, wield sound, travel the astral, and heal what you once believed was too broken to touch. And here you are: still breathing, still transforming, still walking toward the light within you. This book may be coming to a close, but your remembering is just beginning. God and You is not the end of a story—it is a threshold to your own.

You are the key. You are the bridge. You are the living temple of sacred intelligence and unconditional love. You have the power to, and actively do, co-create with God.

Now you are being invited into something deeper—your own direct experience of God, not just in stillness or prayer. Not just in a healing room or dreamscape, but in every moment, every breath, every interaction.

God is in your hands that serve. God is in your voice that forgives. God is in the space you hold for others when they cannot yet hold it for themselves.

So, what now?

Now you embody the divine.

You speak the truth that trembles on your tongue for you know it leads to your liberation. You forgive what aches and forgive what you may have forgotten. You walk the Earth as a full embodiment of God. You activate others not by force, but by frequency. And when you forget—because we all do—you come back to these pages, these truths, these echoes of the Infinite. A remembrance of the true essence of you.

If you are willing, I invite you to say it with me one more time:

"Divine Holy Spirit, Father-Mother God, I don't know what to do with all this information, but I am willing to learn."

Let this be your next step, your next prayer. Then be still and know…

God is all that is, all you are, and everything in between.

Acknowledgments

To my family and friends— I love you. To my mom, Roza, for her unwavering love, immense strength, and steadfast determination. To my father, Benson, thank you for showing me that love has no boundaries, for teaching us unity and the importance of family. You both gave everything you had to raise daughters who could stand in their truth, walk with integrity, and carry light into the world.

To my sisters, Jessica and Nasike, your strength, your brilliance, and your love have shaped me in more ways than words could ever fully express. I love you both endlessly. Thank you for being my sisters, my mirrors, and my home.

Jessica, my big sister, your fierce determination and unwavering truth have been a guiding light. You've taught me how to stand tall, hold my position, and never shrink to make others comfortable. Your boldness, your loyalty, and your fire remind me every day that the only voice that truly matters is the one within. Thank you for showing me what it means to own your power unapologetically.

Nasike, my little sister—my little one and forever soul friend—you are the embodiment of grace, intelligence, humor, and heart. Watching you become a doctor, healing and saving lives, has been one of the greatest honors of my life. Your compassion, grounding energy, and light bring healing not just to your patients, but to all who know you, including me.

Glossary of Sacred Terms

Below is a glossary of sacred or metaphysical terms used throughout this book.

Akashic Records – A multidimensional library of every soul's thoughts, emotions, experiences, and choices throughout all timelines. Often accessed through meditation or altered states of consciousness

Ascension – The process of raising one's vibrational frequency to align with higher states of awareness, unconditional love, and divine truth. It's not about leaving Earth, but anchoring Heaven through embodied presence

Astral Realm – The energetic plane between the physical and spiritual dimensions. This is where the soul travels during dreams or out-of-body experiences

Aura – The electromagnetic field of energy that surrounds all living beings. It reflects one's physical, emotional, mental, and spiritual state. The aura can change on a daily basis depending on the person's state of being

Chakra – Energy centers in the body that govern specific emotional, physical, and spiritual aspects

Clairsenses – Psychic senses. Includes clairvoyance (seeing), clairaudience (hearing), clairsentience (feeling), claircognizance (knowing), clairalience (smelling), and clairgustance (tasting)

Consciousness – The awareness of self, others, and the greater unified field. In this book, "God's consciousness" refers to the infinite divine intelligence that permeates all things

Divine Feminine/Divine Masculine – Archetypal energies that exist within all beings, regardless of gender. The Divine Feminine is receptive, nurturing, intuitive; the Divine Masculine is active, structured, protective. True healing integrates both

Download/Divine Download – A spontaneous transmission of divine insight, understanding, or energetic frequency from higher realms into your awareness or body

Energy Work – A healing modality that works with the body's subtle energy fields to clear blockages, raise vibration, and support holistic healing. Reiki is one example

Ether – The fifth element in ancient traditions, representing the spiritual or unseen realm that connects all other elements. Often referred to as the "spiritual fabric" of the cosmos

Fascia – Connective tissue in the body that holds emotional and energetic imprints. Often considered a physical doorway to stored trauma and cellular memory

Frequency – The measurable vibration or rate at which energy moves. Higher frequencies are associated with love, clarity, and expansion; lower with fear, shame, and contraction

God – Referred to in this book as the Source of All That Is, unconditional love, divine intelligence, and the original spark of creation. Not confined to a specific religion or form

Gridwork – The act of working with Earth's energetic ley lines or grid systems to anchor light, codes, or healing into the land and collective field

Higher Self – The eternal, divine part of your soul that exists beyond ego and time. It is your truest Self, often accessed through meditation or intuition

Initiation – A life experience or spiritual process that activates a higher level of soul awareness. Often includes challenges meant to catalyze growth and remembrance

Karma – The energetic law of cause and effect. Not punishment, but an opportunity to learn, balance, and evolve through experiences and soul contracts

Ley Lines – Invisible energy lines that crisscross the Earth, often connecting sacred sites. These energetic meridians carry planetary codes and spiritual potential

Lightbody – The energetic counterpart to the physical body, composed of light and multidimensional geometry. It activates as consciousness expands

Light Language – A multidimensional soul language beyond human dialects. Carries frequencies for healing, activation, and remembrance. Often spoken, sung, or written in symbols

Merkaba – A sacred geometric structure, often seen as two interlocked tetrahedrons spinning in opposite directions. Represents the union of body, spirit, and light

Numerology – The metaphysical study of numbers and their vibrational meanings. Each number carries archetypal energy that reflects divine patterns and soul guidance

Portal – An energetic doorway to higher consciousness, timelines, or divine frequencies. Can be physical (a place), temporal (a date), or internal (a meditative state)

Reiki – A Japanese energy healing technique that channels universal life force energy through the hands to support physical, emotional, and spiritual healing

Sacred Geometry – Divine patterns and shapes found throughout nature and the universe that reflect the mathematical order of creation (e.g., Flower of Life, Golden Ratio)

Shadow – The unconscious or suppressed parts of the self that carry unhealed pain, fear, or shame. Shadow work is the practice of integrating these parts with love

Solfeggio Frequencies – Ancient healing sound tones used to tune the body and soul to natural harmonics of the universe

Soul Contract – Agreements made by your soul before incarnation to learn, teach, or support others through specific experiences or relationships

Spirit Guide – Non-physical beings of light who assist, protect, and guide you on your soul path. Can be ancestors, angels, or star beings

Third Eye – The sixth chakra located between the brows, associated with inner vision, intuition, and clairvoyance

Timeline – A vibrational path of experience based on the choices and frequencies you align with. We shift timelines as our consciousness evolves

Transmission – A flow of divine energy, wisdom, or codes shared through a person's words, presence, or vibration

Vibration – The frequency at which something exists or resonates. Everything in existence vibrates, and your vibration influences what you attract and create

White Flame Consciousness – A divine state of purity, unity, and remembrance of your eternal connection to Source. It's associated with Christ consciousness and the highest light codes of God